Poets of the Confederation

Carman/Lampman/Roberts/Scott

Edited and with an introduction by Malcolm Ross

M&S

All the poems reproduced in this book are copyrighted works and permission
to reprint any one of them should be sought from the copyright owners with
whose kind permission they are reproduced here. These sources are as
follows: *Sir Charles G. D. Roberts: Selected Poems*, edited and with an
introduction by Desmond Pacey, The Ryerson Press, 1955; *The Selected
Poems of Bliss Carman*, edited and with an introduction by Lorne Pierce,
McClelland and Stewart Limited, 1954; *Selected Poems of Archibald
Lampman*, chosen and with a memoir by Duncan Campbell Scott, The
Ryerson Press, 1947; *The Poems of Duncan Campbell Scott*, McClelland and
Stewart, Limited, 1926; *Selected Poems of Duncan Campbell Scott*, with a
memoir by E. K. Brown, The Ryerson Press, 1954.

Canadian Cataloguing in Publication Data

Main entry under title:

Poets of the Confederation

(New Canadian library ; N1)
(Poets of Canada ; v.1)
ISBN 0-7710-9501-5

1. Canadian poetry (English) – 19th century.*
2. Canadian poetry (English) – 20th century.*
I. Ross, Malcolm, 1911–   . II. Series: New Canadian
library ; no. 1. III. Series: Poets of Canada ; v. 1.

PS8289.P64 1987   C811'.4'08   C87-095129-7
PR9195.6.P64 1987

Manufactured in Canada by Webcom Limited

McClelland & Stewart Inc.
The Canadian Publishers
481 University Avenue
Toronto, Ontario
M5G 2E9

CONTENTS

iii

INTRODUCTION

It is fair enough, I think, to call Roberts, Carman, Lampman, and Scott our "Confederation Poets." Not that they were avowed and self-conscious prophets of the new Canadian nationalism. Roberts, it is true, had his fling at the "patriotic ode," but it is precisely this part of his work which one would most willingly let die. Charles Mair, perhaps, is our Confederation poet in the obvious political sense—the trouble being that he simply was not a poet. Our men *were* poets—at their best, good poets. And what is surely remarkable when one recalls our earlier cultural history, these men stood at the head of a lively company of compatriots, who, if not "good poets," at least managed to write a considerable number of good poems (one thinks of W. W. Campbell, Isabella Valency Crawford, Theodore Goodridge Roberts, Marjorie Pickthall, Francis Sherman).

The point is that Roberts gave proof that we had a voice, that "the child of nations, giant-limb'd" was not a deaf mute after all. And the editors, preachers, and bookish lawyers who had been clamouring ever since 1867 for a sign that we were indeed a people and not just the jagged fabrication of a parliamentary act, had, by the 1880's, some real reason to rejoice. One remembers, here, Archibald Lampman's excitement over Roberts's first volume of poetry. It is, says Lampman, "a wonderful thing that such a work could be done by a Canadian ... *one of ourselves.*"

A new note, certainly. Only a few years had elapsed since it was even technically possible to call a New Brunswicker like Roberts "a Canadian." This is significant enough. Even more significant is the fact that Lampman is excited not because Roberts, in *Orion,* writes a "Canadian poem" (he does not) but because Roberts *is* a Canadian and nevertheless can write! For Lampman "had been under the depressing conviction that we were situated hopelessly on the outskirts of civilization where no literature or art could be, and that it was useless to expect that anything great could be done by any of our companions, still more useless to expect that we could do it ourselves. I sat up most of the night reading and rereading *Orion* in a state of the wildest excitement, and when I went to bed I could not sleep."

Should we smile indulgently at such boyish extravagance? That word "great," for instance. Surely *Orion* gave no proof that "greatness" was now within our reach. Yet after (just after) Heavysege, just after Sangster, just after Mair, *Orion* must have seemed much more mighty than it seems, at this distance, to us. Here, at least, was skill, the possession of the craft, the mystery. Here was *another*—one like oneself. Here was something stirring, something in a book "by one of ourselves," something as alive and wonderful in its own way as the words on the lips of the railway builders. Our empty landscape of the mind was being peopled at last. *Orion* proved to Lampman that this high landscape could be linked by a stronger, surer steel than John A. and Van Horne could ever lay down. Lampman exulted because he was no longer alone. And it was no longer "useless to expect that we could do it ourselves."

Lampman's note on *Orion* makes the right entry to the work of the whole Confederation group. Unquestionably Lampman here reflects the peculiar national spirit of the immediate post-Confederation period. This was a nationalism in search of a nation and Lampman, in his way, like Macdonald in his, learned which way to look. There is even a hint of "Canada First" in Lampman's excited pride of discovery. But it is an echo at some remove. No political statement, no practical pointers, nothing faintly like a manifesto. The air is charged, that is all. And the poet suddenly finds that he too can draw breath in this air. There will be no Whitmanesque gestures, no tub-thumping 100 per cent Canadianism. Even Roberts in his posture of national laureate is as much imperialist as nationalist. And even in Toronto he remains a New Brunswicker with one eye on London, the other on New York.

Canada does not have, did not have, will not have writers as specifically and identifiably Canadian as Whitman and Hemingway are specifically and identifiably American. Our leap from colony to nation was accomplished without revolution, without a sharp cultural and ideological break from Europe, without the fission and fusion of Civil War. Roberts and Carman learn as happily from Emerson and Royce as from Browning, Rossetti, and Verlaine. And Darwin is made to take on the look of a Miramichi backwoodsman! True, Lampman and Roberts suddenly find that they are Canadians. But they are also (and at the same time) thoroughgoing provincials (with a feeling for place), and thoroughgoing citizens of the world (with a feeling for time).

Our group of Confederation Poets is important for us (among other reasons) because already it shows forth the peculiar and inevitable "openness" of the Canadian culture. Indeed, our best writers today have much more in common with Roberts and the others than they would care to admit. It is natural enough that our recent writers have abandoned and disparaged "The Maple Leaf School" of Canadian poetry. Fashions have changed. Techniques have changed. But the changes have not really been ours—at least, we have not been the innovators. Our newest poets owe as much to Eliot, Auden, and Robert Graves as the Confederation Poets owed to the seminal writers of their day. The point is—the debt is assimilated now (as it was then) and therefore is *almost* paid back. Then as now the feeling for place checks and balances the feeling for time. Then as now, voices are heard with individual accent (Lampman, Layton, Carman, Klein—not one of them sits on the ventriloquist's knee).

With Roberts and his group, then, the broad design of our unique, inevitable, and precarious cultural pattern emerges. This pattern, by the force of historical and geographical circumstances, is a pattern of opposites in tension. From the very first there is, of course, the federal-regional tension. (Roberts is suddenly "one of ourselves." He is—and yet he is not.) There is also, inescapably, the American-British tension. (One remembers the pull of Emerson and Royce against the English Victorians. And one remembers Roberts's break from Goldwin Smith over the question of our "North Americanism." We had to be British *and* American at once if we were to be Canadian. . . .) There is (and always was) the French-English tension, affecting very little the poetic imagination of Roberts and Carman but evident to a degree in the work of Lampman and Scott,

Our poetry just after Confederation ceased to be *merely* regional and therefore could be *unashamedly* regional. One could be, with all one's heart, the singer of the parish if one could be sure of a hearing beyond the parish. The appearance of national magazines like *The Canadian Monthly, The Nation,* and Goldwin Smith's *The Week* let the local voices out. These magazines, and notably *The Week,* also provided the necessary link with the literary and intellectual life of New York and London. Thus all the shaping forces—regional, national, and international—were now at play. The separate (and rudimentary) colonial cultures of British North America had been caught up and transfigured in a new (if tentative and precarious) structure. Within this structure all the original elements remained alive and operative.

Obviously there were (and are) dangers in the peculiarly Canadian cultural situation. These tugs and pulls we have been considering do not and cannot guarantee equilibrium and "settled character." It is not only the case that Roberts is least Canadian when he tries to write a deliberately "national" poetry. It is also clear that while he is responsive to the fashionable religious and philosophical ideas of the late nineteenth century he tends to recite them rather than to use them poetically. His philosophical poems, like most of Carman's, are little more than second-hand ideas versified. This is not to say that a poet's "ideas" must be "original." But they must be experienced, incarnated. One suspects that the crosswinds of regional, national, and international impulse flurried Roberts and that he never really found his own poetic centre. The fatal temptation of the Canadian poet (then as now) is to write "over his head," to simulate, and to improvise à la mode. The philosophical poems of Roberts and Carman stand as warnings to us. It is well to reach out beyond the parish for the idea. But the idea must be made flesh—flesh of our flesh. For if parochialism has been our curse so has its opposite. The task for us has always been to find the centre.

Roberts repays study—for his failures as much as for his successes. One finds in him wonderful flashes of wit (as in "Philander's Song"); evidences of pure religious feeling (as in "When Mary the Mother Kissed the Child"); an engaging fancy (as in "The Unknown City"); above all, the painter's eye, as in the homely *Songs of the Common Day.* The elements of a major poetry are here, and they are here still to be enjoyed—and praised. The pity is that these elements were never fused in the single "emotive furnace."

Carman is a less complicated creature than Roberts and much less conscious of his Canadianism. He was seduced as easily as Roberts by the second-hand idea and in later years his talent was dissipated in the pursuit of quite ludicrous "metaphysical" will-o'-the-wisps. Nevertheless Carman has an utterly individual voice. In his very early work like the "Low Tide on Grand Pré" and even in later volumes like the *Sappho* and *Pipes of Pan* he strikes a note of magic the like of which has never been heard in the land before or since. He cannot be called a "national poet." But his delicate, eerie seascapes and his lonely cadences will continue to haunt the Canadian imagination.

It is astonishing how unlike Roberts Carman really is—although without Roberts and the crosswinds of the post-Confederation years, Carman might not have written poetry at all. While we have tended at times to lump together all these Confederation poets as "landscape painters," it is nevertheless the fact that no one of these men could be mistaken for the other and, with the possible exception of Roberts in his simpler descriptive pieces, no one of these men is concerned with description for its own sake.

Carman is a lyrical impressionist whose images project ecstatic feeling. Duncan Campbell Scott, at his most typical, constructs fantasy or uses his landscape as a tragic stage for the dark human figures who seem to rise out of it. Lampman, it is true, has the camera eye. But Lampman is no mere photographer. With Scott (and more completely than Scott), he has, poetically, met the demands of his place and his time. He has all the regional poet's feeling for place. We have already noticed his feeling for the wider place—the nation—and we can guess what this meant to his energy as a poet. Like Roberts (and more intensively than Roberts) he searches for the idea, the philosopher's stone. He searches not in the abstract but in time, his time. And he searches within the self (as Roberts failed to do).

It is not just that in poems like "The City of the End of Things" and "Epitaph on a Rich Man" Lampman seems to have a social and political insight absent in his fellows. It is that he never appropriates an idea for mere recitation. Ideas are germinal for him, infecting the tissues of his thought, now driven off, now recalled, realized or discharged. His poems, even his "nature" poems, are tense with the shadows of opposite values. Like the existentialist of our day, Lampman is not so much "in search of himself" as engaged strenuously in the creation of the self. Every idea is approached as potentially the substance of a "clearer self" in the making. Even landscape is made into a symbol of the deep, interior processes of the self in motion, or is used, like the hypnotist's bauble, to induce a sett-

xi

ling of the troubled surfaces of the mind and a miraculous transparency which opens into the depths. Thus the superb "landscape" poem "Heat" concludes:

> And yet to me not this or that
> Is always sharp or always sweet;
> In the sloped shadow of my hat
> I lean at rest, and drain the heat;
> Nay more, I think some blessèd power
> Hath brought me wandering idly here:
> *In the full furnace of the hour*
> *My thoughts go keen and clear*

(Italics mine)

The purpose of this volume is to give the general reader a fuller selection of the four "large" Confederation Poets than is available in any of the current anthologies. It is not possible in such a short space to make an adequate critical comment on each (or any) of these poets. A brief critical bibliography is therefore appended. My hope is that the selection here presented will remind us that we possess a poetic tradition of considerable merit and of recognizable character—a tradition which endures because, as Canadians, we cannot and should not want to escape the conditions which shaped it and us.

Malcolm Ross
Queen's University
Kingston, Ontario

    . . . SUDDEN the day
Brake full. The healing of its radiance fell
Upon his eyes, and straight his sightless eyes
Were opened. All the morning's majesty
And mystery of loveliness lay bare
Before him; all the limitless blue sea
Brightening with laughter many a league around,
Wind-wrinkled, keel-uncloven, far below;
And far above the bright sky-neighbouring peaks;
And all around the broken precipices,
Cleft-rooted pines swung over falling foam,
And silver vapours flushed with the wide flood
Of crimson slanted from the opening east
Well ranked, the vanguard of the day—all these
Invited him, but these he heeded not.
For there beside him, veiléd in a mist
Where—through the enfolded splendour issued forth—
As delicate music unto one asleep
Through mist of dreams flows softly—all her hair
A mist of gold flung down about her feet,
Her dewy, cool, pink fingers parting it
Till glowing lips, and half-seen snowy curves
Like Parian stone, unnerved him, waited SHE—
Than Circe skilfuller to put away
His pain, to set his sorrow afar off—
Eos, with warm heart warm for *him*. His toils
Endured in vain, his great deeds wrought in vain,
His bitter pain, Œnopion's house accurst,
And even his sweet revenge, he recked not of;
But gave his heart up straightway unto love.

SUMMERS and summers have come, and gone with the
    flight of the swallow;
Sunshine and thunder have been, storm, and winter, and
    frost;
Many and many a sorrow has all but died from remem-
    brance,
Many a dream of joy fall'n in the shadow of pain.
Hands of chance and change have marred, or moulded,
    or broken,
Busy with spirit or flesh, all I most have adored;
Even the bosom of Earth is strewn with heavier shadows—
Only in these green hills, aslant to the sea, no change!
Here where the road that has climbed from the inland
    valleys and woodlands,
Dips from the hill-tops down, straight to the base of the
    hills—
Here, from my vantage-ground, I can see the scattering
    houses,
Stained with time, set warm in orchards, meadows and
    wheat,
Dotting the broad bright slopes outspread to southward
    and eastward,
Wind-swept all day long, blown by the south-east wind.

Skirting the sunbright uplands stretches a riband of
    meadow,
Shorn of the labouring grass, bulwarked well from the sea,
Fenced on its seaward border with long clay dikes from
    the turbid
Surge and flow of the tides vexing the Westmoreland
    shores.
Yonder, toward the left, lie broad the Westmoreland
    marshes—
Miles on miles they extend, level, and grassy, and dim,
Clear from the long red sweep of flats to the sky in the
    distance,
Save for the outlying heights, green-rampired Cumber-
    land Point;
Miles on miles outrolled, and the river-channels divide
    them—
Miles on miles of green, barred by the hurtling gusts.

Miles on miles beyond the tawny bay is Minudie.
There are the low blue hills; villages gleam at their feet.
Nearer a white sail shines across the water, and nearer
Still are the slim, grey masts of fishing boats dry on the
flats.

Ah, how well I remember those wide red flats, above
tide-mark
Pale with scurf of the salt, seamed and baked in the sun!
Well I remember the piles of blocks and ropes, and the
net-reels
Wound with the beaded nets, dripping and dark from the
sea!
Now at this season the nets are unwound; they hang
from the rafters
Over the fresh-stowed hay in upland barns, and the wind
Blows all day through the chinks, with the streaks of
sunlight, and sways them
Softly at will; or they lie heaped in the gloom of a loft.

Now at this season the reels are empty and idle; I see
them
Over the lines of the dikes, over the gossiping grass.
Now at this season they swing in the long strong wind,
thro' the lonesome
Golden afternoon, shunned by the foraging gulls.
Near about sunset the crane will journey homeward
above them;
Round them, under the moon, all the calm night long,
Winnowing soft grey wings of marsh-owls wander and
wander,
Now to the broad, lit marsh, now to the dusk of the dike.
Soon, thro' their dew-wet frames, in the live keen fresh-
ness of morning,
Out of the teeth of the dawn blows back the awakening
wind.
Then, as the blue day mounts, and the low-shot shafts
of the sunlight
Glance from the tide to the shore, gossamers jewelled
with dew
Sparkle and wave, where late sea-spoiling fathoms of
drift-net
Myriad-meshed, uploomed sombrely over the land.

Well I remember it all. The salt raw scent of the margin;
While, with men at the windlass, groaned each reel, and
    the net,
Surging in ponderous lengths, uprose and coiled in its
    station;
Then each man to his home—well I remember it all!

Yet, as I sit and watch, this present peace of the land-
    scape—
Stranded boats, these reels empty and idle, the hush,
One grey hawk slow-wheeling above yon cluster of hay-
    stacks—
More than the old-time stir this stillness welcomes me
    home.
Ah the old-time stir, how once it stung me with rapture—
Old-time sweetness, the winds freighted with honey and
    salt!
Yet will I stay my steps and not go down to the marsh-
    land—
Muse and recall far off, rather remember than see—
Lest on too close sight I miss the darling illusion,
Spy at their task even here the hands of chance and
    change.

THE SOWER

A BROWN, sad-coloured hillside, where the soil,
Fresh from the frequent harrow, deep and fine,
Lies bare; no break in the remote sky-line,
Save where a flock of pigeons streams aloft,
Startled from feed in some low-lying croft,
Of far-off spires with yellow of sunset shine;
And here the Sower, unwittingly divine,
Exerts the silent forethought of his toil.

Alone he treads the glebe, his measured stride
Dumb in the yielding soil; and though small joy
Dwell in his heavy face, as spreads the blind
Pale grain from his dispensing palm aside,
This plodding churl grows great in his employ—
Godlike, he makes provision for mankind.

THE POTATO HARVEST

A HIGH bare field, brown from the plough, and borne
Aslant from sunset; amber wastes of sky
Washing the ridge; a clamour of crows that fly
In from the wide flats where the spent tides mourn
To yon their rocking roosts in pines wind-torn;
A line of grey snake-fence, that zigzags by
A pond and cattle; from the homestead nigh
The long deep summonings of the supper horn.

Black on the ridge, against that lonely flush,
A cart, and stoop-necked oxen; ranged beside,
Some barrels; and the day-worn harvest-folk,
Here, emptying their baskets, jar the hush
With hollow thunders. Down the dusk hillside
Lumbers the wain; and day fades out like smoke.

THE SALT FLATS

HERE clove the keels of centuries ago
Where now unvisited the flats lie bare.
Here seethed the sweep of journeying waters, where
No more the tumbling floods of Fundy flow,
And only in the samphire pipes creep slow
The salty currents of the sap. The air
Hums desolately with wings that seaward fare,
Over the lonely reaches beating low.

The wastes of hard and meagre weeds are thronged
With murmurs of a past that time has wronged;
And ghosts of many an ancient memory
Dwell by the brackish pools and ditches blind,
In these low-lying pastures of the wind,
These marshes pale and meadows by the sea.

THE PEA-FIELDS

THESE are the fields of light, and laughing air,
And yellow butterflies, and foraging bees,
And whitish, wayward blossoms winged as these,
And pale green tangles like a seamaid's hair.
Pale, pale the blue, but pure beyond compare,
And pale the sparkle of the far-off seas,
A-shimmer like these fluttering slopes of peas,
And pale the open landscape everywhere.

From fence to fence a perfumed breath exhales
O'er the bright pallor of the well-loved fields—
My fields of Tantramar in summer-time;
And, scorning the poor feed their pasture yields,
Up from the bushy lots the cattle climb,
To gaze with longing through the grey, mossed rails.

the tended gan.

THE MOWING

THIS is the voice of high midsummer's heat.
The rasping vibrant clamour soars and shrills
O'er all the meadowy range of shadeless hills,
As if a host of giant cicadae beat
The cymbals of their wings with tireless feet,
Or brazen grasshoppers with triumphing note
From the long swath proclaimed the fate that smote
The clover and timothy-tops and meadowsweet.

The crying knives glide on; the green swath lies.
And all noon long the sun, with chemic ray,
Seals up each cordial essence in its cell,
That in the dusky stalls, some winter's day,
The spirit of June, here prisoned by his spell,
May cheer the herds with pasture memories.

THE WINTER FIELDS

WINDS here, and sleet, and frost that bites like steel.
The low bleak hill rounds under the low sky.
Naked of flock and fold the fallows lie,
Thin streaked with meagre drift. The gusts reveal
By fits the dim grey snakes of fence, that steal
Through the white dusk. The hill-foot poplars sigh,
While storm and death with winter trample by,
And the iron fields ring sharp, and blind lights reel.

Yet in the lonely ridges, wrenched with pain,
Harsh solitary hillocks, bound and dumb,
Brave glebes close-lipped beneath the scourge and chain,
Lurks hid the germ of ecstasy—the sum
Of life that waits on summer, till the rain
Whisper in April and the crocus come.

IN THE WIDE AWE
AND
WISDOM OF THE NIGHT

IN THE wide awe and wisdom of the night
I saw the round world rolling on its way,
Beyond significance of depth or height,
Beyond the interchange of dark and day.
I marked the march to which is set no pause,
And that stupendous orbit, round whose rim
The great sphere sweeps, obedient unto laws
That utter the eternal thought of Him.

I compassed time, outstripped the starry speed,
And in my still soul apprehended space,
Till, weighing laws which these but blindly heed,
At last I came before Him face to face—
And knew the Universe of no such span
As the august infinitude of Man.

MARSYAS

A LITTLE grey hill-glade, close-turfed, withdrawn
Beyond resort or heed of trafficking feet,
Ringed round with slim trunks of the mountain ash.
Through the slim trunks and scarlet bunches flash—
Beneath the clear chill glitterings of the dawn—
Far off, the crests, where down the rosy shore
The Pontic surges beat.
The plains lie dim below. The thin airs wash
The circuit of the autumn-coloured hills,
And this high glade, whereon
The satyr pipes, who soon shall pipe no more.
He sits against the beech-tree's mighty bole—
He leans, and with persuasive breathing fills
The happy shadows of the slant-set lawn.
The goat-feet fold beneath a gnarlèd root;
And sweet, and sweet the note that steals and thrills
From slender stops of that shy flute.

Then to the goat-feet comes the wide-eyed fawn
Hearkening; the rabbits fringe the glade, and lay
Their long ears to the sound;
In the pale boughs the partridge gather round,
And quaint hern from the sea-green river reeds;
The wild ram halts upon a rocky horn
O'erhanging; and, unmindful of his prey,
The leopard steals with narrowed lids to lay
His spotted length along the ground.
The thin airs wash, the thin clouds wander by,
And those hushed listeners move not.   All the morn
He pipes, soft-swaying, and with half-shut eye,
In rapt content of utterance —
                              nor heeds
The young God standing in his branchy place,
The languor on his lips, and in his face,
Divinely inaccessible, the scorn.

EPITAPH FOR A SAILOR BURIED ASHORE

HE WHO but yesterday would roam
Careless as clouds and currents range,
In homeless wandering most at home,
Inhabiter of change;

Who wooed the west to win the east,
And named the stars of North and South,
And felt the zest of Freedom's feast
Familiar in his mouth;
Who found a faith in stranger-speech,
And fellowship in foreign hands,
And had within his eager reach
The relish of all lands—

How circumscribed a plot of earth
Keeps now his restless footsteps still,
Whose wish was wide as ocean's girth,
Whose will the water's will!

OUT OF the dreams that heap
The hollow hand of sleep—
Out of the dark sublime,
From the averted Face
Beyond the bournes of space,
Into the sudden sun
We journey, one by one.
Out of the hidden shade
Wherein desire is made—
Out of the pregnant stir
Where death and life confer—
The dark and mystic heat
Where soul and matter meet—
The enigmatic Will—
We start, and then are still.

Inexorably decreed
By the ancestral deed,
The puppets of our sires,
We work out blind desires,
And for our sons ordain,
The blessing or the bane.
In ignorance we stand
With fate on either hand,
And question stars and earth
Of life, and death, and birth.
With wonder in our eyes
We scan the kindred skies,
While through the common grass
Our atoms mix and pass.
We feel the sap go free
When spring comes to the tree;
And in our blood is stirred
What warms the brooding bird.
The vital fire we breathe
That bud and blade bequeath,
And strength of native clay
In our full veins hath sway.

But in the urge intense
And fellowship of sense,
Suddenly comes a word
In other ages heard.
On a great wind our souls
Are borne to unknown goals,
And past the bournes of space
To the unaverted Face.

THE UNSLEEPING

I SOOTHE to unimagined sleep
The sunless bases of the deep.
And then I stir the aching tide
That gropes in its reluctant side.

I heave aloft the smoking hill;
To silent peace its throes I still.
But ever at its heart of fire
I lurk, an unassuaged desire.

I wrap me in the sightless germ
An instant or an endless term;
And still its atoms are my care,
Dispersed in ashes or in air.

I hush the comets one by one
To sleep for ages in the sun;
The sun resumes before my face
His circuit of the shores of space.

The mount, the star, the germ, the deep,
They all shall wake, they all shall sleep.
Time, like a flurry of wild rain,
Shall drift across the darkened pane.

Space, in the dim predestined hour,
Shall crumble like a ruined tower.
I only, with unfaltering eye,
Shall watch the dreams of God go by.

RECESSIONAL

NOW ALONG the solemn heights
Fade the Autumn's altar-lights;
Down the great earth's glimmering chancel
Glide the days and nights.

Little kindred of the grass,
Like a shadow in a glass
Falls the dark and falls the stillness;
We must rise and pass.

We must rise and follow, wending
Where the nights and days have ending—
Pass in order pale and slow
Unto sleep extending.

Little brothers of the clod,
Soul of fire and seed of sod,
We must fare into the silence
At the knees of God.

Little comrades of the sky
Wing to wing we wander by,
Going, going, going, going,
Softly as a sigh.

Hark, the moving shapes confer,
Globe of dew and gossamer,
Fading and ephemeral spirits
In the dusk astir.

Moth and blossom, blade and bee,
Worlds must go as well as we,
In the long procession joining
Mount, and star, and sea.

Toward the shadowy brink we climb
Where the round year rolls sublime,
Rolls, and drops, and falls forever
In the vast of time;

Like a plummet plunging deep
Past the utmost reach of sleep,
Till remembrance has no longer
Care to laugh or weep.

BESIDE THE WINTER SEA

AS ONE who sleeps, and hears across his dream
The cry of battles ended long ago,
Inland I hear the calling of the sea.
I hear its hollow voices, though between
My wind-worn dwelling and thy wave-worn strand
How many miles, how many mountains are!
And thou beside the winter sea alone
Art walking, with thy cloak about thy face.
Bleak, bleak the tide, and evening coming on;
And grey the pale, pale light that wans thy face.
Solemnly breaks the long wave at thy feet;
And sullenly in patches clings the snow
Upon the low, red rocks worn round with years.
I see thine eyes, I see their grave desire,
Unsatisfied and lonely as the sea's—
Yet how unlike the wintry sea's despair!
For could my feet but follow thine, my hands
But reach for thy warm hands beneath thy cloak,
What summer joy would lighten in thy face,
What sunshine warm thine eyes, and thy sad mouth
Break to a dewy rose and laugh on mine!

THE WITCHES' FLIGHT

COME, Red Mouse,
And come, Black Cat!
Oh, see what the goat
And the toad are at!
Oh, see them where
They rise in the air,
And wheel and dance
With the whirling bat!

We rise, we rise
On the smoking air;
And the withered breast
Grows young and fair;
And the eyes grow bright
With alluring light,
And the fierce mouth softens
With love's soft prayer.

Come, White Sisters,
Naked of limb!
The horned moon reddens;
The stars grow dim;
The crags in the gloom
Of our caldron's fume
Shudder and topple
And reel and swim.

We mount, we mount
Till the moon seems nigh.
Our rout possesses
The middle sky.

With strange embraces,
And maddened faces,
And streaming tresses,
We twist and fly.

Come, White Sisters,
And four-foot kin,
For the horned moon sinks
And the reek grows thin,
And brief is the night
Of our delight,
And brief the span
Of our secret sin.

BEFORE the feet of the dew
There came a call I knew,
Luring me into the garden
Where the tall white lilies grew.

I stood in the dusk between
The companies of green,
O'er whose aerial ranks
The lilies rose serene.

And the breathing air was stirred
By an unremembered word,
Soft, incommunicable—
And wings not of a bird.

I heard the spent blooms sighing,
The expectant buds replying;
I felt the life of the leaves,
Ephemeral, yet undying.

The spirits of earth were there,
Thronging the shadowed air,
Serving among the lilies,
In an ecstasy of prayer.

Their speech I could not tell;
But the sap in each green cell,
And the pure initiate petals,
They knew that language well.

I felt the soul of the trees—
Of the white, eternal seas—
Of the flickering bats and night-moths
And my own soul kin to these.

And a spell came out of space
From the light of its starry place,
And I saw in the deep of my heart
The image of God's face.

THE SOLITARY WOODSMAN

WHEN the grey lake-water rushes
Past the dripping alder bushes,
And the bodeful autumn wind
In the fir-tree weeps and hushes—

When the air is sharply damp
Round the solitary camp,
And the moose-bush in the thicket
Glimmers like a scarlet lamp—

When the birches twinkle yellow,
And the cornel bunches mellow,
And the owl across the twilight
Trumpets to his downy fellow—

When the nut-fed chipmunks romp
Through the maples' crimson pomp,
And the slim viburnum flushes
In the darkness of the swamp—

When the blueberries are dead,
When the rowan clusters red,
And the shy bear, summer-sleekened,
In the bracken makes his bed—

On a day there comes once more
To the latched and lonely door,
Down the wood-road striding silent,
One who has been here before.

Green spruce branches for his head,
Here he makes his simple bed,
Couching with the sun, and rising
When the dawn is frosty red.

All day long he wanders wide
With the grey moss for his guide,
And his lonely axe-stroke startles
The expectant forest-side.

Toward the quiet close of day
Back to camp he takes his way,
And about his sober footsteps
Unafraid the squirrels play.

On his roof the red leaf falls,
At his door the bluejay calls,
And he hears the wood-mice hurry
Up and down his rough log walls;

Hears the laughter of the loon
Thrill the dying afternoon—
Hears the calling of the moose
Echo to the early moon.

And he hears the partridge drumming,
The belated hornet humming—
All the faint, prophetic sounds
That foretell the winter's coming.

And the wind about his eaves
Through the chilly night-wet grieves,
And the earth's dumb patience fills him,
Fellow to the falling leaves.

FAR UP the lonely strand the storm had lifted her.
And now along her keel the merry tides make stir
No more. The running waves that sparkled at her prow
Seethe to the chains and sing no more with laughter now.
No more the clean sea-furrow follows her. No more
To the hum of her gallant tackle the hale Nor'-westers
    roar.
No more her bulwarks journey. For the only boon they
    crave
Is the guerdon of all good ships and true, the boon of a
    deep-sea grave.

> *Take me out, sink me deep in the green profound,*
> *To sway with the long weed, swing with the drowned,*
> *Where the change of the soft tide makes no sound,*
> *Far below the keels of the outward bound.*

No more she mounts the circles from Fundy to the Horn,
From Cuba to the Cape runs down the tropic morn,
Explores the Vast Uncharted where great bergs ride in
    ranks,
Nor shouts a broad "Ahoy" to the dories on the Banks.
No more she races freights to Zanzibar and back,
Nor creeps where the fog lies blind along the liners' track,
No more she dares the cyclone's disastrous core of calm
To greet across the dropping wave the amber isles of palm.

> *Take me out, sink me deep in the green profound,*
> *To sway with the long weed, swing with the drowned,*
> *Where the change of the soft tide makes no sound,*
> *Far below the keels of the outward bound.*

Amid her trafficking peers, the wind-wise, journeyed ships,
At the black wharves no more, nor at the weedy slips,
She comes to port with cargo from many a storied clime.
No more to the rough-throat chantey her windlass creaks
    in time.
No more she loads for London with spices from Ceylon—
With white spruce deals and wheat and apples from St.
    John.
No more from Pernambuco with coffee-bags—no more
With hides from Buenos Ayres she clears for Baltimore.

Take me out, sink me deep in the green profound,
To sway with the long weed, swing with the drowned,
Where the change of the soft tide makes no sound,
Far below the keels of the outward bound.

Wan with the slow vicissitudes of wind and rain and sun
How grieves her deck for the sailors whose hearty brawls
    are done!
Only the wandering gull brings word of the open wave,
With shrill scream at her taffrail deriding her alien grave.
Around the keel that raced the dolphin and the shark
Only the sand-wren twitters from barren dawn till dark;
And all the long blank noon the blank sand chafes and
    mars
The prow once swift to follow the lure of the dancing
    stars.

Take me out, sink me deep in the green profound,
To sway with the long weed, swing with the drowned,
Where the change of the soft tide makes no sound,
Far below the keels of the outward bound.

And when the winds are low, and when the tides are still,
And the round moon rises inland over the naked hill,
And o'er her parching seams the dry cloud-shadows pass,
And dry along the land-rim lie the shadows of thin grass,
Then aches her soul with longing to launch and sink
    away
Where the fine silts lift and settle, the sea-things drift and
    sway,
To make the port of Last Desire, and slumber with her
    peers
In the tide-wash rocking softly through the unnumbered
    years.

Take me out, sink me deep in the green profound,
To sway with the long weed, swing with the drowned,
Where the change of the soft tide makes no sound,
Far below the keels of the outward bound.

WHEN MARY THE MOTHER
KISSED THE CHILD

WHEN Mary the Mother kissed the Child
And night on the wintry hills grew mild,
And the strange star swung from the courts of air
To serve at a manger with kings in prayer,
Then did the day of the simple kin
And the unregarded folk begin.

When Mary the Mother forgot the pain,
In the stable of rock began love's reign.
When that new light on their grave eyes broke
The oxen were glad and forgot their yoke;
And the huddled sheep in the far hill fold
Stirred in their sleep and felt no cold.

When Mary the Mother gave of her breast
To the poor inn's latest and lowliest guest—
The God born out of the woman's side—
The Babe of Heaven by Earth denied—
Then did the hurt ones cease to moan,
And the long-supplanted came to their own.

When Mary the Mother felt faint hands
Beat at her bosom with life's demands,
And nought to her were the kneeling kings,
The serving star and the half-seen wings,
Then was the little of earth made great,
And the man came back to the God's estate.

THE PLACE OF HIS REST

THE green marsh-mallows
Are over him.
Along the shallows
The pale lights swim.

Wide air, washed grasses,
And waveless stream;
And over him passes
The drift of dream;—

The pearl-hue down
Of the poplar seed;
The elm-flower brown;
And the sway of the reed;

The blue moth, winged
With a flake of sky;
The bee, gold ringed;
And the dragon-fly.

Lightly the rushes
Lean to his breast;
A bird's wing brushes
The place of his rest.

The far-flown swallow,
The gold-finch flame—
They come, they follow
The paths he came.

'Tis the land of No Care
Where now he lies,
Fulfilled the prayer
Of his weary eyes,

And while around him
The kind grass creeps,
Where peace hath found him
How sound he sleeps.

Well to his slumber
Attends the year:
Soft rains without number
Soft noons, blue clear,

With nights of balm,
And the dark, sweet hours
Brooding with calm,
Pregnant with flowers.

See how she speeds them,
Each childlike bloom,
And softly leads them
To tend his tomb!

The white-thorn nears
As the cowslip goes;
Then the iris appears;
And then, the rose.

THE UNKNOWN CITY

THERE lies a city inaccessible,
Where the dead dreamers dwell.

Abrupt and blue, with many a high ravine
And soaring bridge half seen,
With many an iris cloud that comes and goes
Over the ancient snows,
The imminent hills environ it, and hold
Its portals from of old,
That grief invade not, weariness, nor war.
Nor anguish evermore.

White-walled and jettied on the peacock tide,
With domes and towers enskied,
Its battlements and balconies one sheen
Of ever-living green,
It hears the happy dreamers turning home
Slow-oared across the foam.

Cool are its streets with waters musical
And fountains shadowy fall.
With orange and anemone and rose
And every flower that blows
Of magic scent or unimagined dye,
Its gardens shine and sigh.
Its chambers, memoried with old romance
And faëry circumstance—
From any window love may lean some time
For love that dares to climb.

This is that city babe and seer divined
With pure, believing mind.
This is the home of unachieved emprise.
Here, here the visioned eyes
Of them that dream past any power to do,
Wake to the dream come true.
Here the high failure, not the level fame,
Attests the spirit's aim.
Here is fulfilled each hope that soared and sought
Beyond the bournes of thought.

The obdurate marble yields; the canvas glows;
Perfect the column grows;
The chorded cadence art could ne'er attain
Crowns the imperfect strain;
And the great song that seemed to die unsung
Triumphs upon the tongue.

PHILANDER'S SONG

I sat and read Anacreon.
Moved by the gay, delicious measure
I mused that lips were made for love,
And love to charm a poet's leisure.

And as I mused a maid came by
With something in her look that caught me.
Forgotten was Anacreon's line,
But not the lesson he had taught me.

THE SUN goes down, and over all
These barren reaches by the tide
Such unelusive glories fall,
I almost dream they yet will bide
Until the coming of the tide.

And yet I know that not for us,
By an ecstasy of dream,
He lingers to keep luminous Sun
A little while the grievous stream,
Which frets, uncomforted of dream—

A grievous stream, that to and fro
Athrough the fields of Acadie
Goes wandering, as if to know
Why one beloved face should be
So long from home and Acadie.

Was it a year or lives ago
We took the grasses in our hands,
And caught the summer flying low
Over the waving meadow lands,
And held it there between our hands?

The while the river at our feet—
A drowsy inland meadow stream—
At set of sun the after-heat
Made running gold, and in the gleam
We freed our birch upon the stream.

There down along the elms at dusk
We lifted dripping blade to drift,
Through twilight scented fine like musk,
Where night and gloom awhile uplift,
Nor sunder soul and soul adrift.

And that we took into our hands
Spirit of life or subtler thing—
Breathed on us there, and loosed the bands
Of death, and taught us, whispering,
The secret of some wonder-thing.

Then all your face grew light, and seemed
To hold the shadow of the sun;
The evening faltered, and I deemed
That time was ripe, and years had done
Their wheeling underneath the sun.

So all desire and all regret,
And fear and memory, were naught;
One to remember or forget
The keen delight our hands had caught;
Morrow and yesterday were naught.

The night has fallen, and the tide. . .
Now and again comes drifting home,
Across these aching barrens wide,
A sigh like driven wind or foam:
In grief the flood is bursting home.

A WINDFLOWER

BETWEEN the roadside and the wood,
Between the dawning and the dew,
A tiny flower before the sun,
Ephemeral in time, I grew.

And there upon the trail of spring,
Not death nor love nor any name
Known among men in all their lands
Could blur the wild desire with shame.

But down my dayspan of the year
The feet of straying winds came by;
And all my trembling soul was thrilled
To follow one lost mountain cry.

And then my heart beat once and broke
To hear the sweeping rain forebode
Some ruin in the April world,
Between the woodside and the road.

Tonight can bring no healing now;
The calm of yesternight is gone;
Surely the wind is but the wind,
And I a broken waif thereon.

A SEA CHILD

THE LOVER of child Marjory
Had one white hour of life brim full;
Now the old nurse, the rocking sea,
Hath him to lull.

The daughter of child Marjory
Hath in her veins, to beat and run,
The glad indomitable sea,
The strong white sun.

THE EAVESDROPPER

IN A still room at hush of dawn
My love and I lay side by side
And heard the roaming forest wind
Stir in the paling autumn-tide.

I watched her earth-brown eyes grow glad
Because the round day was so fair;
While memories of reluctant night
Lurked in the blue dusk of her hair.

Outside, a yellow maple tree,
Shifting upon the silvery blue
With tiny multitudinous sound,
Rustled to let the sunlight through.

The livelong day the elfish leaves
Danced with their shadows on the floor;
And the lost children of the wind
Went straying homeward by our door.

And all the swarthy afternoon
We watched the great deliberate sun
Walk through the crimsoned hazy world,
Counting his hilltops one by one.

Then as the purple twilight came
And touched the vines along our eaves,
Another Shadow stood without
And gloomed the dancing of the leaves.

The silence fell on my Love's lips;
Her great brown eyes were veiled and sad
With pondering some maze of dream,
Though all the splendid year was glad.

Restless and vague as a grey wind
Her heart had grown, she knew not why.
But hurrying to the open door,
Against the verge of western sky

I saw retreating on the hills,
Looming and sinister and black,
The stealthy figure swift and huge
Of One who strode and looked not back.

THE JOYS OF THE ROAD

NOW the joys of the road are chiefly these:
A crimson touch on the hard-wood trees;

A vagrant's morning wide and blue,
In early fall, when the wind walks, too;

A shadow, highway cool and brown,
Alluring up and enticing down

From rippled water to dappled swamp,
From purple glory to scarlet pomp;

The outward eye, the quiet will,
And the striding heart from hill to hill;

The tempter apple over the fence;
The cobweb bloom on the yellow quince;

The palish asters along the wood—
A lyric touch of the solitude;

An open hand, an easy shoe,
And a hope to make the day go through—

Another to sleep with, and a third
To wake me up at the voice of a bird;

The resonant far-listening morn,
And the hoarse whisper of the corn;

The crickets mourning their comrades lost
In the night's retreat from the gathering frost;

(Or is it their slogan, plaintive and shrill,
As they beat on their corselets, valiant still?)

A hunger fit for the kings of the sea
And a loaf of bread for Dickon and me;

A thirst like that of the Thirsty Sword,
And a jug of cider on the board;

An idle noon, a bubbling spring,
The sea in the pine-tops murmuring;

A scrap of gossip at the ferry;
A comrade neither glum nor merry,

Asking nothing, revealing naught,
But minting his words from a fund of thought,

A keeper of silence eloquent,
Needy, yet royally well content,

Of the mettled breed, yet abhorring strife,
And full of the mellow juice of life,

A taster of wine, with an eye for a maid,
Never too bold, and never afraid,

Never heart-whole, never heart-sick,
(These are the things I worship in Dick)

No fidget and no reformer, just
A calm observer of ought and must.

A lover of books, but a reader of man,
No cynic and no charlatan,

Who never defers, and never demands,
But, smiling, takes the world in his hands—

Seeing it good as when God first saw
And gave it the weight of His will for law.

And O the joy that is never won,
But follows and follows the journeying sun,

By marsh and tide, by meadow and stream,
A will-o'-the-wind, a light-o'-dream,

Delusion afar, delight anear,
From morrow to morrow, from year to year,

A jack-o'-lantern, a fairy fire,
A dare, a bliss, and a desire!

The racy smell of the forest loam,
When the stealthy, sad-heart leaves go home;

(O leaves, O leaves, I am one with you,
Of the mould and the sun and the wind and the dew!)

The broad gold wake of the afternoon;
The silent fleck of the cold new moon;

The sound of the hollow sea's release
From stormy tumult to starry peace;

With only another league to wend;
And two brown arms at the journey's end!

These are the joys of the open road—
For him who travels without a load.

AN AUTUMN SONG

THERE is something in the autumn that is native to my blood,
Touch of manner, hint of mood;
And my heart is like a rhyme,
With the yellow and the purple and the crimson keeping time.

The scarlet of the maples can shake me like a cry
Of bugles going by.
And my lonely spirit thrills
To see the frosty asters like smoke upon the hills.

There is something in October sets the gipsy blood astir:
We must rise and follow her,
When from every hill aflame
She calls and calls each vagabond by name.

BUIE ANNAJOHN

BUIE ANNAJOHN was the king's black mare,
Buie, Buie, Buie Annajohn!
 Satin was her coat and silk was her hair.
Buie Annajohn,
The young king's own.
March with the white moon, march with the sun,
March with the merry men, Buie Annajohn!

Buie Annajohn, when the dew lay hoar,
(Buie, Buie, Buie Annajohn!)
Down through the meadowlands went to war—
Buie Annajohn,
The young king's own.
March by the river road, march by the dune,
March with the merry men, Buie Annajohn!

Buie Annajohn had the heart of flame,
Buie, Buie, Buie Annajohn!
First of the hosts to the hostings came
Buie Annajohn,

The young king's own.
March till we march the red sun down,
March with the merry men, Buie Annajohn!

Back from the battle at the close of day,
(Buie, Buie, Buie Annajohn!)
Came with the war cheers, came with a neigh,
Buie Annajohn,
The young king's own.
Oh, heavy was the sword that we laid on;
But half of the heave was Buie Annajohn,
Buie, Buie, Buie Annajohn!

BEHIND THE ARRAS

I LIKE the old house tolerably well,
Where I must dwell
Like a familiar gnome;
And yet I never shall feel quite at home.
I love to roam.

Day after day I loiter and explore
From door to door;
So many treasures lure
The curious mind. What histories obscure
They must immure!

I hardly know which room I care for best;
This fronting west,
With the strange hills in view,
Where the great sun goes,—where I may go too,
When my lease is through,—

Or this one for the morning and the east,
Where a man may feast
His eyes on looming sails,
And be the first to catch their foreign hails
Or spy their bales

Then the pale summer twilights towards the pole
It thrills my soul
With wonder and delight,
When gold-green shadows walk the world at night,
So still, so bright.

There at the window many a time of year,
Strange faces peer,
Solemn though not unkind,
Their wits in search of something left behind
Time out of mind;

As if they once had lived here, and stole back
To the window crack
For a peep which seems to say,
"Good fortune, brother, in your house of clay!"
And then, "Good day!"

I hear their footsteps on the gravel walk,
Their scraps of talk,
And hurrying after, reach
Only the crazy sea-drone of the beach
In endless speech.

And often when the autumn noons are still,
By swale and hill
I see their gipsy signs,
Trespassing somewhere on my border lines;
With what designs?

I forth afoot; but when I reach the place,
Hardly a trace,
Save the soft purple haze
Of smouldering camp-fires, any hint betrays
Who went these ways.

Or tatters of pale aster blue, descried
By the roadside,
Reveal whither they fled;
Or the swamp maples, here and there a shred
Of Indian red.

But most of all, the marvellous tapestry
Engrosses me,
Where such strange things are rife,
Fancies of beasts and flowers, and love and strife,
Woven to the life;

Degraded shapes and splendid seraph forms,
And teeming swarms
Of creatures gauzy dim
That cloud the dusk, and painted fish that swim,
At the weaver's whim;

And wonderful birds that wheel and hang in the air;
And beings with hair,
And moving eyes in the face,
And white bone teeth and hideous grins, who race
From place to place;

They build great temples to their John-a-nod,
And fume and plod
To deck themselves with gold,
And paint themselves like chattels to be sold,
Then turn to mould.

Sometimes they seem almost as real as I;
I hear them sigh;
I see them bow with grief,
Or dance for joy like any aspen leaf;
But that is brief.

They have mad wars and phantom marriages;
Nor seem to guess
There are dimensions still,
Beyond thought's reach, though not beyond love's will,
For soul to fill.

And some I call my friends, and make believe
Their spirits grieve,
Brood, and rejoice with mine;
I talk to them in phrases quaint and fine
Over the wine;

I tell them all my secrets; touch their hands;
One understands
Perhaps. How hard he tries
To speak! And yet those glorious mild eyes,
His best replies!

Ceaseless and daft and terrible and blind,
Like a lost mind.
I often chill with fear
When I bethink me, What if it should peer
At my shoulder here!

Perchance he drives the merry-go-round whose track
Is the zodiac;
His name is No-man's-friend;
And his gabbling parrot-talk has neither trend,
Beginning, nor end.

A prince of madness too, I'd cry, "A rat!"
And lunge thereat,—
Let out at one swift thrust
The cunning arch-delusion of the dust
I so mistrust,

But that I fear I should disclose a face
Wearing the trace
Of my own human guise,
Piteous, unharmful, loving, sad, and wise,
With the speaking eyes.

I would the house were rid of his grim pranks,
Moaning from banks
Of pine trees in the moon,
Startling the silence like a demoniac loon
At dead of noon.

Or whispering his fool-talk to the leaves
About my eaves.
And yet how can I know
Tis not a happy Ariel masking so
In mocking woe?

Then with a little broken laugh I say,
Snatching away
The curtain where he grinned
 (My feverish sight thought) like a sin unsinned,
"Only the wind!"

Yet often too he steals so softly by,
With half a sigh,
I deem he must be mild,
Fair as a woman, gentle as a child,
And forest wild.

Passing the door where an old wind-harp swings,
With its five strings,
Contrived long years ago
By my first predecessor bent to show
His handcraft so,

He lays his fingers on the aeolian wire,
As a core of fire
Is laid upon the blast
To kindle and glow and fill the purple vast
Of dark at last.

I even have my cronies, one or two,
My cherished few.
But ah, they do not stay!
For the sun fades them and they pass away,
As I grow gray.

Yet while they last how actual they seem!
Their faces beam;
I give them all their names,
Bertram and Gilbert, Louis, Frank and James,
Each with his aims;

One thinks he is a poet, and writes verse
His friends rehearse;
Another is full of law;
A third sees pictures which his hand can draw
Without a flaw.

Strangest of all, they never rest. Day long
They shift and throng,
Moved by invisible will,
Like a great breath which puffs across my sill,
And then is still;

It shakes my lovely manikins on the wall;
Squall after squall,
Gust upon crowding gust,
It sweeps them willy nilly like blown dust
With glory or lust.

It is the world-ghost, the time-spirit, come
None knows wherefrom,
The viewless draughty tide
And wash of being. I hear it yaw and glide,
And then subside,

Along these ghostly corridors and halls
Like faint footfalls;
The hangings stir in the air;
And when I start and challenge, "Who goes there?"
It answers, "Where?"

The wail and sob and moan of the sea's dirge,
Its plangor and surge;
The awful biting sough
Of drifted snows along some arctic bluff,
That veer and luff,

And have the vacant boding human cry,
As they go by;—
Is it a banished soul
Dredging the dark like a distracted mole
Under a knoll?

Like some invisible henchman old and gray,
Day after day
I hear it come and go,
With stealthy swift unmeaning to and fro,
Muttering low,

Weird wise and low, piercing and keen and glad,
Or dim and sad
As a forgotten strain
Born when the broken legions of the rain
Swept through the plain—

He plays, like some dread veiled mysteriarch,
Lighting the dark,
Bidding the spring grow warm,
The gendering merge and loosing of spirit in form,
Peace out of storm.

For music is the sacrament of love;
He broods above
The virgin silence, till
She yields for rapture shuddering, yearning still
To his sweet will.

I hear him sing, "Your harp is like a mesh,
Woven of flesh
And spread within the shoal
Of life, where runs the tide-race of the soul
In my control.

"Though my wild way may ruin what it bends,
It makes amends
To the frail downy clocks,
Telling their seed a secret that unlocks
The granite rocks.

"The womb of silence to the crave of sound
Is heaven unfound,
Till I, to soothe and slake
Being's most utter and imperious ache,
Bid rhythm awake.

"If with such agonies of bliss, my kin,
I enter in
Your prison house of sense,
With what a joyous freed intelligence
I shall go hence."

I need no more to guess the weaver's name,
Nor ask his aim,
Who hung each hall and room
With swarthy-tinged vermilion upon gloom;
I know that loom.

Give me a little space and time enough,
From ravelings rough
I could revive, reweave,
A fabric of beauty art might well believe
Were past retrieve.

O men and women in that rich design,
Sleep-soft, sun-fine,
Dew-tenuous and free,
A tone of the infinite wind-themes of the sea,
Borne in to me,

Reveals how you were woven to the might
Of shadow and light.
You are the dream of One
Who loves to haunt and yet appears to shun
My door in the sun;

As the white roving sea tern fleck and skim
The morning's rim;
Or the dark thrushes clear
Their flutes of music leisurely and sheer,
Then hush to hear.

I know him when the last red brands of day
Smoulder away,
And when the vernal showers
Bring back the heart to all my valley flowers
In the soft hours.

O hand of mine and brain of mine, be yours,
While time endures,
To acquiesce and learn!
For what we best may dare and drudge and yearn,
Let soul discern.

So, fellows, we shall reach the gusty gate,
Early or late,
And part without remorse,
A cadence dying down unto its source
In music's course;

You to the perfect rhythms of flowers and birds,
Colors and words,
The heart-beats of the earth,
To be remoulded always of one worth
From birth to birth;

I to the broken rhythm of thought and man,
The sweep and span
Of memory and hope
About the orbit where they still must grope
For wider scope,

To be through thousand springs restored, renewed,
With love imbrued,
With increments of will
Made strong, perceiving unattainment still
From each new skill.

Always the flawless beauty, always the chord
Of the Overword,
Dominant, pleading, sure,
No truth too small to save and make endure.
No good too poor !

And since no mortal can at last disdain
That sweet refrain,
But lets go strife and care,
Borne like a strain of bird notes on the air,
The wind knows where;

Some quiet April evening soft and strange,
When comes the change
No spirit can deplore.
I shall be one with all I was before,
In death once more.

A SON OF THE SEA

I was born for deep-sea faring;
I was bred to put to sea;
Stories of my father's daring
Filled me at my mother's knee.

I was sired among the surges;
I was cubbed beside the foam;
All my heart is in its verges,
And the sea wind is my home.

All my boyhood, from far vernal
Bourns of being, came to me
Dream-like, plangent, and eternal
Memories of the plunging sea.

THE GRAVEDIGGER

Oh, the shambling sea is a sexton old,
And well his work is done.
With an equal grave for lord and knave,
He buries them every one.

Then hoy and rip, with a rolling hip,
He makes for the nearest shore;
And God, who sent him a thousand ship,
Will send him a thousand more;
But some he'll save for a bleaching grave,
And shoulder them in to shore—
And shoulder them in, shoulder them in,
Shoulder them in to shore.

Oh, the ships of Greece and the ships of Tyre
Went out, and where are they?
In the port they made, they are delayed
With the ships of yesterday.

He followed the ships of England far,
As the ships of long ago;
And the ships of France they led him a dance,
But he laid them all arow.

Oh, a loafing idle lubber to him
Is the sexton of the town;
For sure and swift, with a guiding lift,
He shovels the dead men down.

But though he delves so fierce and grim,
His honest graves are wide,
As well they know who sleep below
The dredge of the deepest tide.

Oh, he works with a rollicking stave at lip,
And loud is the chorus skirled;
With the burly note of his rumbling throat
He batters it down the world.

He learned it once in his father's house,
Where the ballads of eld were sung;
And merry enough is the burden rough,
But no man knows the tongue.

Oh, fair, they say, was his bride to see,
And wilful she must have been,
That she could bide at his gruesome side
When the first red dawn came in.

And sweet, they say, is her kiss to those
She greets to his border home;
And softer than sleep her hand's first sweep
That beckons, and they come.

Oh, crooked is he, but strong enough
To handle the tallest mast;
From the royal barque to the slaver dark,
He buries them all at last.

Then hoy and rip, with a rolling hip,
He makes for the nearest shore;
And God, who sent him a thousand ship,
Will send him a thousand more;

But some he'll save for a bleaching grave,
And shoulder them in to shore—
Shoulder them in, shoulder them in,
Shoulder them in to shore.

THE DEAD FAUN

WHO HATH done this thing? What wonder is this that lies
On the green earth so still under purple skies,
Like a hyacinth shaft the careless mower has cut
And thought of no more?

Who hath wrought this pitiful wrong on the lovely earth?
What ruthless hand could ruin that harmless mirth?
O heart of things, what undoing is here, never now
To be mended more!

No more, O beautiful boy, shall thy fleet feet stray
Through the cool beech wood on the shadowy mountain way,
Nor halt by the well at noon, nor trample the flowers
On the forest floor.

Thy beautiful light-seeing gold-green eyes, so glad
When day came over the hill, so wondrous sad
When the burning sun went slowly under the sea,
Shall look no more.

Thy nimble fingers that plucked the fruit from the bough,
Or fondled the nymph's bright hair and filleted brow,
Or played the wild mellow pipe of thy father Pan,
Shall play no more.

The sensitive ears that knew all the speech of the wood,
Every call of the birds and the creatures, and understood
What the wind to the water said, what the river replied,
Shall hear no more.

Thy scarlet and lovely mouth which the dryads knew,
Dear whimsical ardent mouth that love spoke through,
For all the kisses of life that it took and gave.
Shall say no more.

The wind may whisper to him, he will heed no more;
The leaves may murmur and lisp, he will laugh no more;
The oreads weep and be heavy at heart for him,
He will care no more.

The reverberant thrushes may peal from the hemlock glooms,
The summer clouds be woven on azure looms;
He is done with all lovely things of earth forever
And ever more.

FROM EARTH'S LYRIC

• • •

THE BANDS of Arcturus are slackened;
Orion goes forth from his place
On the slopes of the night, leading homeward
His hound from the chase.

The Pleiades weary and follow
The dance of the ghostly dawn;
The revel of silence is over;
Earth's lyric comes on.

A golden flute in the cedars,
A silver pipe in the swales,
And the slow large life of the forest
Wells back and prevails.

A breath of the woodland spirit
Has blown out the bubble of spring
To this tenuous hyaline glory
One touch sets swing.

THE SCEPTICS

SAID Grass, "What is that sound
So dismally profound,
That detonates and desolates the air?"

"That is St. Peter's bell,"
Said rain-wise Pimpernel;
"He is music to the godly,
Though to us he sounds so oddly,
And he terrifies the faithful unto prayer."

Said Grass, "And whither track
These creatures all in black,
So woebegone and penitent and meek?"

"They're mortals bound for church,"
Said the little Silver Birch;
"They hope to get to heaven
And have their sins forgiven,
If they talk to God about it once a week."

Said Grass, "What is that noise
That startles and destroys
Our blessed summer brooding when we're tired?"

"That's folk a-praising God,"
Said the tough old cynic Clod;
"They do it every Sunday,
They'll be all right on Monday;
It's just a little habit they've acquired."

THE LAST ROOM

THERE, close the door!
I shall not need these lodgings any more.
Now that I go, dismantled wall and floor
Reproach me and deplore.

"How well," they say,
"And silently we served you day by day—
Took every mood, as you were sad or gay
In that strange mortal way."

These patient walls
Seem half to know what suffering befalls
The steadfast soul whom destiny appals
And circumstance enthralls.

A solitude,
Dim as an orchard, quiet as a wood;
My six mute friends who stolidly withstood
Tempest and turmoil rude;

One door, where through
Came human love in little gown and shoe;
One window, where great Nature robed in blue
Smiled benediction too;

And one hearthstone,
The kind primeval fire-god made his own—
Bringing us back the wood life we had known,
With lighted log and cone.

Here life was spent
To glorify one mortal tenement,
Where freedom turned the key on discontent
And bade the world relent.

With one farewell
I leave you now, with not a word to tell
Where comedy and moonshine used to dwell
Within a brick-built cell.

In days to be
Others shall laugh here, roister and make free,
Be bold or gay—but no such comedy
As blessed this life for me.

In nights to come
Others shall dream here, radiant or glum,
Pondering the book God gives us each to thumb—
Our page to solve and sum—

But nevermore
Such moonshine as would tread this square of floor,
And for love's sake illumine and explore
The dark at sorrow's core.

"The sad Pierrot
Lived here and loved"—how will the story go?—
"Caught rapture from the moment's zest or woe,
One winter long ago.

"Here did Pierrette
Throw dice with destiny to pay love's debt,
Gay, kind and fearless, without one regret
When the last stake was set."

Peace, peace, fair room—
My peace be with them still, through shine and gloom,
Who here may sojourn, ere they too resume
This search for house and home.

Now, to explore!
The impatient wind is in the corridor;
Fate lays a finger on my sleeve once more;
And I must close this door.

LOVE, BY THAT LOOSENED HAIR

LOVE, by that loosened hair,
Well now I know
Where the lost Lilith went
So long ago.

Love, by those starry eyes
I understand
How the sea maidens lure
Mortals from land.

Love, by that welling laugh
Joy claims its own
Sea-born and wind-wayward
Child of the sun.

ONCE YOU LAY UPON MY BOSOM

ONCE you lay upon my bosom
While the long blue-silver moonlight
Walked the plain, with that pure passion
    All your own.

Now the moon is gone, the Pleiads
Gone, the dead of night is going;
Slips the hour, and on my bed
    I lie alone.

WILL NOT MEN REMEMBER US

WILL not men remember us
In the days to come hereafter—
Thy warm-coloured loving beauty
    And my love for thee?

Thou, the hyacinth that grows
By a quiet-running river;
I, the watery reflection
    And the broken gleam.

SOFTER THAN THE HILL-FOG
TO THE FOREST

SOFTER than the hill-fog to the forest
Are the loving hands of my dear lover,
When she sleeps beside me in the starlight
And her beauty drenches me with rest.

As the quiet mist enfolds the beech-trees,
Even as she dreams her arms enfold me,
Half awaking with a hundred kisses
On the scarlet lily of her mouth.

HOW SOON WILL ALL MY LOVELY
DAYS BE OVER

HOW SOON will all my lovely days be over,
And I no more be found beneath the sun—
Neither beside the many-murmuring sea,
Nor where the plain-winds whisper to the reeds,
Nor in the tall beech-woods among the hills
Where roam the bright-lipped Oreads, nor along
The pasture-sides where berry-pickers stray
And harmless shepherds pipe their sheep to fold!

For I am eager, and the flame of life
Burns quickly in the fragile lamp of clay.
Passion and love and longing and hot tears
Consume this mortal Sappho, and too soon
A great wind from the dark will blow upon me,
And I be no more found in the fair world,
For all the search of the revolving moon
And patient shine of everlasting stars.

I LOVED THEE, ATTHIS, IN THE LONG AGO

I LOVED thee, Atthis, in the long ago,
When the great oleanders were in flower
In the broad herded meadows full of sun.
And we would often at the fall of dusk
Wander together by the silver stream,
When the soft grass-heads were all wet with dew
And purple-misted in the fading light.
And joy I knew and sorrow at thy voice,
And the superb magnificence of love—
The loneliness that saddens solitude,
And the sweet speech that makes it durable—
The bitter longing and the keen desire,
The sweet companionship through quiet days
In the slow ample beauty of the world,
And the unutterable glad release
Within the temple of the holy night.
O Atthis, how I loved thee long ago
In that fair perished summer by the sea!

OVER THE ROOFS
THE HONEY-COLOURED MOON

OVER the roofs the honey-coloured moon,
With purple shadows on the silver grass,

And the warm south-wind on the curving sea,
While we two, lovers past all turmoil now,

Watch from the window the white sails come in,
Bearing what unknown ventures safe to port!

So falls the hour of twilight and of love
With wizardry to loose the hearts of men,

And there is nothing more in this great world
Than thou and I, and the blue dome of dusk.

LIKE A TALL FOREST
WERE THEIR SPEARS

LIKE a tall forest were their spears,
Their banners like a silken sea,
When the great host in splendour passed
Across the crimson sinking sun.

And then the bray of brazen horns
Arose above their clanking march,
As the long waving column filed
Into the odorous purple dusk.

O lover, in this radiant world
Whence is the race of mortal men,
So frail, so mighty, and so fond,
That fleets into the vast unknown?

AT THE GREAT RELEASE

WHEN the black horses from the house of Dis
Stop at my door and the dread charioteer
Knocks at my portal, summoning me to go
On the far solitary unknown way
Where all the race of men fare and are lost,
Fleeting and numerous as the autumnal leaves
Before the wind in Lesbos of the Isles;

Though a chill draught of fear may quell my soul
And dim my spirit like a flickering lamp
In the great gusty hall of some old king,
Only one mordant unassuaged regret,
One passionate eternal human grief,
Would wring my heart with bitterness and tears
And set the mask of sorrow on my face.

Not youth, nor early fame, nor pleasant days,
Nor flutes, nor roses, nor the taste of wine,
Nor sweet companions of the idle hour
Who brought me tender joys, nor the glad sound
Of children's voices playing in the dusk;
All these I could forget and bid good-bye
And pass to my oblivion nor repine.

Nor the green woods that I so dearly love,
Nor summer hills in their serenity,
Nor the great sea mystic and musical,
Nor drone of insects, nor the call of birds,
Nor soft spring flowers, nor the wintry stars;
To all the lovely earth that was my home
Smiling and valiant I could say farewell.

But not, O not to one strong little hand,
To one droll mouth brimming with witty words,
Nor ever to the unevasive eyes
Where dwell the light and sweetness of the world
With all the sapphire sparkle of the sea!
Ah, Destiny, against whose knees we kneel
With prayer at evening, spare me this one woe!

IF I should tell you I saw Pan lately down by the shallows
    of Silvermine,
Blowing an air on his pipe of willow, just as the moon
    began to shine;
Or say that, coming from town on Wednesday, I met
    Christ walking in Ponus Street;
You might remark, "Our friend is flighty! Visions for
    want of enough red meat!"

Then let me ask you. Last December, when there was
    skating on Wampanaw,
Among the weeds and sticks and grasses under the hard
    black ice I saw
An old mud-turtle poking about, as if he were putting his
    house to rights,
Stiff with the cold perhaps, yet knowing enough to pre-
    pare for the winter nights.

And here he is on a log this morning, sunning himself as
    calm as you please.
But I want to know, when the lock of winter was sprung
    of a sudden, who kept the keys?
Who told old nibbler to go to sleep safe and sound with
    the lily roots,
And then in the first warm days of April—out to the sun
    with the greening shoots?

By night a flock of geese went over, honking north on the
    trails of air,
The spring express—but who despatched it, equipped
    with speed and cunning care?
Hark to our bluebird down in the orchard trolling his
    chant of the happy heart,
As full of light as a theme of Mozart's—but where did he
    learn that more than art?

It matters not though defeat undo me, though faults
  betray me and sorrows scar,
Already I share the life eternal with the April buds and
  the evening star.
The slim new moon is my sister now; the rain, my
  brother; the wind, my friend.
Is it not well with these forever? Can the soul of man
  fare ill in the end?

Archibald Lampman

PALE season, watcher in unvexed suspense,
Still priestess of the patient middle day,
Betwixt wild March's humoured petulance
And the warm wooing of green kirtled May,
Maid month of sunny peace and sober grey,
Weaver of flowers in sunward glades that ring
With murmur of libation to the spring;

As memory of pain, all past, is peace,
And joy, dream-tasted, hath the deepest cheer,
So art thou sweetest of all months that lease
The twelve short spaces of the flying year.
The bloomless days are dead, and frozen fear
No more for many moons shall vex the earth,
Dreaming of summer and fruit-laden mirth.

The grey song-sparrows full of spring have sung
Their clear thin silvery tunes in leafless trees;
The robin hops, and whistles, and among
The silver-tasselled poplars the brown bees
Murmur faint dreams of summer harvestries;
The creamy sun at even scatters down
A gold-green mist across the murmuring town.

By the slow streams the frogs all day and night
Dream without thought of pain or heed of ill,
Watching the long warm silent hours take flight,
And ever with soft throats that pulse and thrill,
From the pale-weeded shallows trill and trill,
Tremulous sweet voices, flute-like, answering
One to another glorying in the spring.

All day across the ever-cloven soil,
Strong horses labour, steaming in the sun,
Down the long furrows with slow straining toil,
Turning the brown clean layers; and one by one
The crows gloom over them till daylight done
Finds them asleep somewhere in duskèd lines
Beyond the wheatlands in the northern pines.

The old year's cloaking of brown leaves, that bind
The forest floor-ways, plated close and true—
The last love's labour of the autumn wind—
Is broken with curled flower buds white and blue

In all the matted hollows, and speared through
With thousand serpent-spotted blades up-sprung,
Yet bloomless, of the slender adder-tongue.

In the warm noon the south wind creeps and cools,
Where the red-budded stems of maples throw
Still tangled etchings on the amber pools,
Quite silent now, forgetful of the slow
Drip of the taps, the troughs, and trampled snow,
The keen March mornings, and the silvering rime
And mirthful labour of the sugar prime.

Ah, I have wandered with unwearied feet,
All the long sweetness of an April day,
Lulled with cool murmurs and the drowsy beat
Of partridge wings in secret thickets grey,
The marriage hymns of all the birds at play,
The faces of sweet flowers, and easeful dreams
Beside slow reaches of frog-haunted streams;

Wandered with happy feet, and quite forgot
The shallow toil, the strife against the grain,
Near souls, that hear us call, but answer not,
The loneliness, perplexity and pain,
And high thoughts cankered with an earthly stain;
And then, the long draught emptied to the lees,
I turn me homeward in slow-pacing ease,

Cleaving the cedar shadows and the thin
Mist of grey gnats that cloud the river shore,
Sweet even choruses, that dance and spin
Soft tangles in the sunset; and once more
The city smites me with its dissonant roar.
To its hot heart I pass, untroubled yet,
Fed with calm hope, without desire or fret.

So to the year's first altar step I bring
Gifts of meek song, and make my spirit free
With the blind working of unanxious spring,
Careless with her, whether the days that flee
Pale drouth or golden-fruited plenty see,
So that we toil, brothers, without distress,
In calm-eyed peace and godlike blamelessness.

THE FROGS

I

BREATHERS of wisdom won without a quest,
Quaint uncouth dreamers, voices high and strange;
Flutists of lands where beauty hath no change,
And wintry grief is a forgotten guest,
Sweet murmurers of everlasting rest,
For whom glad days have ever yet to run,
And moments are as aeons, and the sun
But ever sunken half-way toward the west.

Often to me who heard you in your day,
With close rapt ears, it could not choose but seem
That earth, our mother, searching in what way
Men's hearts might know her spirit's inmost dream;
Ever at rest beneath life's change and stir,
Made you her soul, and bade you pipe for her.

2

In those mute days when spring was in her glee,
And hope was strong, we knew not why or how,
And earth, the mother, dreamed with brooding brow,
Musing on life, and what the hours might be,
When love should ripen to maternity,
Then like high flutes in silvery interchange
Ye piped with voices still and sweet and strange,
And ever as ye piped, on every tree

The great buds swelled; among the pensive woods
The spirits of first flowers awoke and flung
From buried faces the close-fitting hoods,
And listened to your piping till they fell,
The frail spring-beauty with her perfumed bell,
The wind-flower, and the spotted adder-tongue.

3

All the day long, wherever pools might be
Among the golden meadows, where the air
Stood in a dream, as it were moorèd there
For ever in a noon-tide reverie,
Or where the birds made riot of their glee
In the still woods, and the hot sun shone down,
Crossed with warm lucent shadows on the brown
Leaf-paven pools, that bubbled dreamily,

Or far away in whispering river meads
And watery marshes where the brooding noon,
Full with the wonder of its own sweet boon,
Nestled and slept among the noiseless reeds,
Ye sat and murmured, motionless as they,
With eyes that dreamed beyond the night and day.

4

And when day passed and over heaven's height,
Thin with the many stars and cool with dew,
The fingers of the deep hours slowly drew
The wonder of the ever-healing night,
No grief or loneliness or rapt delight
Or weight of silence ever brought to you
Slumber or rest; only your voices grew
More high and solemn; slowly with hushed flight

Ye saw the echoing hours go by, long-drawn,
Nor ever stirred, watching with fathomless eyes,
And with your countless clear antiphonies
Filling the earth and heaven, even till dawn,
Last-risen, found you with its first pale gleam,
Still with soft throats unaltered in your dream.

5

And slowly as we heard you, day by day,
The stillness of enchanted reveries
Bound brain and spirit and half-closèd eyes,
In some divine sweet wonder-dream astray;
To us no sorrow or upreared dismay
Nor any discord came, but evermore
The voices of mankind, the outer roar,
Grew strange and murmurous, faint and far away.

Morning and noon and midnight exquisitely,
Rapt with your voices, this alone we knew,
Cities might change and fall, and men might die,
Secure were we, content to dream with you
That change and pain are shadows faint and fleet,
And dreams are real, and life is only sweet.

HEAT

FROM plains that reel to southward, dim,
The road runs by me white and bare;
Up the steep hill it seems to swim
Beyond, and melt into the glare.
Upward half-way, or it may be
Nearer the summit, slowly steals
A hay-cart, moving dustily
With idly clacking wheels.

By his cart's side the wagoner
Is slouching slowly at his ease,
Half-hidden in the windless blur
Of white dust puffing to his knees.
This wagon on the height above,
From sky to sky on either hand,
Is the sole thing that seems to move
In all the heat-held land.

Beyond me in the fields the sun
Soaks in the grass and hath his will;
I count the marguerites one by one;
Even the buttercups are still.
On the brook yonder not a breath
Disturbs the spider or the midge.
The water-bugs draw close beneath
The cool gloom of the bridge.

Where the far elm-tree shadows flood
Dark patches in the burning grass,
The cows, each with her peaceful cud,
Lie waiting for the heat to pass.
From somewhere on the slope near by
Into the pale depth of the noon
A wandering thrush slides leisurely
His thin revolving tune.

In intervals of dreams I hear
The cricket from the droughty ground;
The grasshoppers spin into mine ear
A small innumerable sound.

I lift mine eyes sometimes to gaze:
The burning sky-line blinds my sight:
The woods far off are blue with haze:
The hills are drenched in light.

And yet to me not this or that
Is always sharp or always sweet;
In the sloped shadow of my hat
I lean at rest, and drain the heat;
Nay more, I think some blessed power
Hath brought me wandering idly here:
In the full furnace of this hour
My thoughts grow keen and clear.

AMONG THE TIMOTHY

LONG hours ago, while yet the morn was blithe,
Nor sharp athirst had drunk the beaded dew,
A mower came, and swung his gleaming scythe
Around this stump, and, shearing slowly, drew
Far round among the clover, ripe for hay,
A circle clean and grey;
And here among the scented swathes that gleam,
Mixed with dead daisies, it is sweet to lie
And watch the grass and the few-clouded sky,
Nor think but only dream.

For when the noon was turning, and the heat
Fell down most heavily on field and wood,
I too came hither, borne on restless feet,
Seeking some comfort for an aching mood.
Ah! I was weary of the drifting hours,
The echoing city towers,
The blind grey streets, the jingle of the throng,
Weary of hope that like a shape of stone
Sat near at hand without a smile or moan,
And weary most of song.

And those high moods of mine that sometime made
My heart a heaven, opening like a flower
A sweeter world where I in wonder strayed,
Begirt with shapes of beauty and the power

Of dreams that moved through that enchanted clime
With changing breaths of rhyme,
Were all gone lifeless now, like those white leaves
That hang all winter, shivering dead and blind
Among the sinewy beeches in the wind,
That vainly calls and grieves.

Ah! I will set no more mine overtaskèd brain
To barren search and toil that beareth nought,
For ever following with sore-footed pain
The crossing pathways of unbournèd thought;
But let it go, as one that hath no skill,
To take what shape it will,
An ant slow-burrowing in the earthy gloom,
A spider bathing in the dew at morn,
Or a brown bee in wayward fancy borne
From hidden bloom to bloom.

Hither and thither o'er the rocking grass
The little breezes, blithe as they are blind,
Teasing the slender blossoms pass and pass,
Soft-footed children of the gipsy wind,
To taste of every purple-fringèd head
Before the bloom is dead;
And scarcely heed the daisies that, endowed
With stems so short they cannot see, up-bear
Their innocent sweet eyes distressed, and stare
Like children in a crowd.

Not far to fieldward in the central heat,
Shadowing the clover, a pale poplar stands
With glimmering leaves that, when the wind comes, beat
Together like innumerable small hands,
And with the calm, as in vague dreams astray,
Hang wan and silver-grey;
Like sleepy maenads, who in pale surprise,
Half-wakened by a prowling beast, have crept
Out of the hidden covert, where they slept,
At noon with languid eyes.

The crickets creak, and through the noonday glow,
That crazy fiddler of the hot mid-year,
The dry cicada plies his wiry bow
In long-spun cadence, thin and dusty sere;

From the green grass the small grasshoppers' din
Spreads soft and silvery thin;
And ever and anon a murmur steals
Into mine ears of toil that moves alway,
The crackling rustle of the pitch-forked hay
And lazy jerk of wheels.

As so I lie and feel the soft hours wane,
To wind and sun and peaceful sound laid bare,
That aching dim discomfort of the brain
Fades off unseen, and shadowy-footed care
Into some hidden corner creeps at last
To slumber deep and fast;
And gliding on, quite fashioned to forget,
From dream to dream I bid my spirit pass
Out into the pale green ever-swaying grass
To brood, but no more fret.

And hour by hour among all shapes that grow
Of purple mints and daisies gemmed with gold
In sweet unrest my visions come and go;
I feel and hear and with quiet eyes behold;
And hour by hour, the ever-journeying sun,
In gold and shadow spun,
Into mine eyes and blood, and through the dim
Green glimmering forest of the grass shines down,
Till flower and blade, and every cranny brown,
And I are soaked with him.

FREEDOM

OUT of the heart of the city begotten
Of the labour of men and their manifold hands,
Whose souls, that were sprung from the earth in her morning,
No longer regard or remember her warning,
Whose hearts in the furnace of care have forgotten
For ever the scent and the hue of her lands;

Out of the heat of the usurer's hold,
From the horrible crash of the strong man's feet;
Out of the shadow where pity is dying;
Out of the clamour where beauty is lying,
Dead in the depth of the struggle for gold;
Out of the din and the glare of the street;

Into the arms of our mother we come,
Our broad strong mother, the innocent earth,
Mother of all things beautiful, blameless,
Mother of hopes that her strength makes tameless,
Where the voices of grief and of battle are dumb,
And the whole world laughs with the light of her mirth.

Over the fields, where the cool winds sweep,
Black with the mould and brown with the loam,
Where the thin green spears of the wheat are appearing,
And the high-ho shouts from the smoky clearing;
Over the widths where the cloud shadows creep;
Over the fields and the fallows we come;

Over the swamps with their pensive noises,
Where the burnished cup of the marigold gleams;
Skirting the reeds, where the quick winds shiver
On the swelling breast of the dimpled river,
And the blue of the kingfisher hangs and poises,
Watching a spot by the edge of the streams;

By the miles of the fences warped and dyed
With the white-hot noons and their withering fires.
Where the rough bees trample the creamy bosoms
Of the hanging tufts of the elder blossoms,
And the spiders weave, and the grey snakes hide,
In the crannied gloom of the stones and the briers;

Over the meadow lands sprouting with thistle,
Where the humming wings of the blackbirds pass,
Where the hollows are banked with the violets flowering,
And the long-limbed pendulous elms are towering,
Where the robins are loud with their voluble whistle,
And the ground-sparrow scurries away through the grass,

Where the restless bobolink loiters and woos
Down in the hollows and over the swells,
Dropping in and out of the shadows,
Sprinkling his music about the meadows,
Whistles and little checks and coos,
And the tinkle of glassy bells;

Into the dim woods full of the tombs
Of the dead trees soft in their sepulchres,
Where the pensive throats of the shy birds hidden,
Pipe to us strangely entering unbidden,
And tenderly still in the tremulous glooms
The trilliums scatter their white-winged stars;

Up to the hills where our tired hearts rest,
Loosen, and halt, and regather their dreams;
Up to the hills, where the winds restore us,
Clearing our eyes to the beauty before us,
Earth with the glory of life on her breast,
Earth with the gleam of her cities and streams.

Here we shall commune with her and no other;
Care and the battle of life shall cease;
Men, her degenerate children, behind us,
Only the might of her beauty shall bind us,
Full of rest, as we gaze on the face of our mother,
Earth in the health and the strength of her peace.

IN OCTOBER

ALONG the waste, a great way off, the pines
Like tall slim priests of storm, stand up and bar
The low long strip of dolorous red that lines
The under west, where wet winds moan afar.
The cornfields all are brown, and brown the meadows
With the blown leaves' wind-heapèd traceries,
And the brown thistle stems that cast no shadows,
And bear no bloom for bees.

As slowly earthward leaf by red leaf slips,
The sad trees rustle in chill misery,
A soft strange inner sound of pain-crazed lips,
That move and murmur incoherently;
As if all leaves, that yet have breath, were sighing,
With pale hushed throats, for death is at the door,
So many low soft masses for the dying
Sweet leaves that live no more.

Here I will sit upon this naked stone,
Draw my coat closer with my numbed hands,
And hear the ferns sigh, and the wet woods moan,
And send my heart out to the ashen lands;
And I will ask myself what golden madness,
What balmèd breaths of dreamland spicery,
What visions of soft laughter and light sadness
Were sweet last month to me.

The dry dead leaves flit by with thin weird tunes,
Like failing murmurs of some conquered creed,
Graven in mystic markings with strange runes,
That none but stars and biting winds may read;
Here I will wait a little; I am weary,
Not torn with pain of any lurid hue,
But only still and very grey and dreary,
Sweet sombre lands, like you.

MIDNIGHT

FROM where I sit, I see the stars,
And down the chilly floor
The moon between the frozen bars
Is glimmering dim and hoar.

Without in many a peakèd mound
The glinting snowdrifts lie;
There is no voice or living sound;
The embers slowly die.

Yet some wild thing is in mine ear;
I hold my breath and hark;
Out of the depth I seem to hear
A crying in the dark;

No sound of man or wife or child,
No sound of beast that groans,
Or of the wind that whistles wild,
Or of the tree that moans:

I know not what it is I hear;
I bend my head and hark:
I cannot drive it from mine ear,
That crying in the dark.

THE KING'S SABBATH

ONCE idly in his hall King Olave sat
Pondering, and with his dagger whittled chips;
And one drew near to him with austere lips,
Saying, "To-morrow is Monday," and at that
The king said nothing, but held forth his flat
Broad palm, and bending on his mighty hips,
Took up and mutely laid thereon the slips
Of scattered wood, as on a hearth, and gat
From off the embers near, a burning brand.
Kindling the pile with this, the dreaming Dane
Sat silent with his eyes set and his bland
Proud mouth, tight-woven, smiling, drawn with pain,
Watching the fierce fire flare, and wax, and wane,
Hiss and burn down upon his shrivelled hand.

THE RAILWAY STATION

THE DARKNESS brings no quiet here, the light
No waking: ever on my blinded brain
The flare of lights, the rush, and cry, and strain,
The engines' scream, the hiss and thunder smite:

I see the hurrying crowds, the clasp, the flight,
Faces that touch, eyes that are dim with pain:
I see the hoarse wheels turn, and the great train
Move labouring out into the bourneless night.
So many souls within its dim recesses,
So many bright, so many mournful eyes:
Mine eyes that watch grow fixed with dreams and guesses;
What threads of life, what hidden histories,
What sweet or passionate dreams and dark distresses,
What unknown thoughts, what various agonies!

IN NOVEMBER

THE HILLS and leafless forests slowly yield
To the thick-driving snow. A little while
And night shall darken down. In shouting file
The woodmen's carts go by me homeward-wheeled,
Past the thin fading stubbles, half concealed,
Now golden-grey, sowed softly through with snow,
Where the last ploughman follows still his row,
Turning black furrows through the whitening field.
Far off the village lamps begin to gleam,
Fast drives the snow, and no man comes this way;
The hills grow wintry white, and bleak winds moan
About the naked uplands. I alone
Am neither sad, nor shelterless, nor grey,
Wrapped round with thought, content to watch and dream.

APRIL IN THE HILLS

TODAY the world is wide and fair
With sunny fields of lucid air,
And waters dancing everywhere;
The snow is almost gone;
The noon is builded high with light,
And over heaven's liquid height,
In steady fleets serene and white,
The happy clouds go on.

The channels run, the bare earth steams,
And every hollow rings and gleams
With jetting falls and dashing streams;
The rivers burst and fill;
The fields are full of little lakes,
And when the romping wind awakes
The water ruffles blue and shakes,
And the pines roar on the hill.

The crows go by, a noisy throng;
About the meadows all day long
The shore-lark drops his brittle song;
And up the leafless tree
The nut-hatch runs, and nods, and clings;
The bluebird dips with flashing wings,
The robin flutes, the sparrow sings,
And the swallows float and flee.

I break the spirit's cloudy bands,
A wanderer in enchanted lands,
I feel the sun upon my hands;
And far from care and strife
The broad earth bids me forth. I rise
With lifted brow and upward eyes.
I bathe my spirit in blue skies,
And taste the springs of life.

I feel the tumult of new birth;
I waken with the wakening earth;
I match the bluebird in her mirth;
And wild with wind and sun,
A treasurer of immortal days,
I roam the glorious world with praise,
The hillsides and the woodland ways,
Till earth and I are one.

AFTER RAIN

FOR three whole days across the sky,
In sullen packs that loomed and broke,
With flying fringes dim as smoke,
The columns of the rain went by;

At every hour the wind awoke;
The darkness passed upon the plain;
The great drops rattled at the pane.

Now piped the wind, or far aloof
Fell to a sough remote and dull;
And all night long with rush and lull
The rain kept drumming on the roof:
I heard till ear and sense were full
The clash or silence of the leaves,
The gurgle in the creaking eaves.

But when the fourth day came—at noon,
The darkness and the rain were by;
The sunward roofs were steaming dry;
And all the world was flecked and strewn
With shadows from a fleecy sky.
The haymakers were forth and gone,
And every rillet laughed and shone.

Then, too, on me that loved so well
The world, despairing in her blight,
Uplifted with her least delight,
On me, as on the earth, there fell
New happiness of mirth and might;
I strode the valleys pied and still;
I climbed upon the breezy hill.

I watched the grey hawk wheel and drop,
Sole shadow on the shining world;
I saw the mountains clothed and curled,
With forest ruffling to the top;
I saw the river's length unfurled,
Pale silver down the fruited plain,
Grown great and stately with the rain.

Through miles of shadow and soft heat,
Where field and fallow, fence and tree,
Were all one world of greenery,
I hear the robin ringing sweet,
The sparrow piping silverly,
The thrushes at the forest's hem;
And as I went I sang with them.

THE SUN CUP

THE EARTH is the cup of the sun,
That he filleth at morning with wine,
With the warm, strong wine of his might
From the vintage of gold and of light,
Fills it, and makes it divine.

And at night when his journey is done,
At the gate of his radiant hall,
He setteth his lips to the brim,
With a long last look of his eye,
And lifts it and draineth it dry,
Drains till he leaveth it all
Empty and hollow and dim.

And then as he passes to sleep,
Still full of the feats that he did
Long ago in Olympian wars,
He closes it down with the sweep
Of its slow-turning luminous lid,
Its cover of darkness and stars,
Wrought once by Hephaestus of old
With violet and vastness and gold.

ALCYONE

IN THE silent depth of space,
Immeasurably old, immeasurably far,
Glittering with a silver flame
Through eternity,
Rolls a great and burning star,
With a noble name,
  Alcyone!

In the glorious chart of heaven
It is marked the first of seven;
'Tis a Pleiad:
And a hundred years of earth
With their long-forgotten deeds have come and gone,

Since that tiny point of light,
Once a splendour fierce and bright,
Had its birth
In the star we gaze upon.
It has travelled all that time—
Thought has not a swifter flight—
Through a region where no faintest gust
Of life comes ever, but the power of night
Dwells stupendous and sublime,
Limitless and void and lonely,
A region mute with age, and peopled only
With the dead and ruined dust
Of worlds that lived eternities ago.
Man! when thou dost think of this,
And what our earth and its existence is,
The half-blind toils since life began,
The little aims, the little span,
With what passion and what pride,
And what hunger fierce and wide,
Thou dost break beyond it all,
Seeking for the spirit unconfined
In the clear abyss of mind
A shelter and a peace majestical.
For what is life to thee,
Turning toward the primal light,
With that stern and silent face,
If thou canst not be
Something radiant and august as night,
Something wide as space?
Therefore with a love and gratitude divine
Thou shalt cherish in thine heart for sign
A vision of the great and burning star,
Immeasurably old, immeasurably far,
Surging forth its silver flame
Through eternity;
And thine inner heart shall ring and cry
With the music strange and high,
The grandeur of its name
    Alcyone!

THE CITY OF THE END OF THINGS

BESIDE the pounding cataracts
Of midnight streams unknown to us
'Tis builded in the leafless tracts
And valleys huge of Tartarus.
Lurid and lofty and vast it seems;
It hath no rounded name that rings,
But I have heard it called in dreams
The City of the End of Things.

Its roofs and iron towers have grown
None knoweth how high within the night,
But in its murky streets far down
A flaming terrible and bright
Shakes all the stalking shadows there,
Across the walls, across the floors,
And shifts upon the upper air
From out a thousand furnace doors;
And all the while an awful sound
Keeps roaring on continually,
And crashes in the ceaseless round
Of a gigantic harmony.
Through its grim depths re-echoing
And all its weary height of walls,
With measured roar and iron ring,
The inhuman music lifts and falls.
Where no thing rests and no man is,
And only fire and night hold sway;
The beat, the thunder and the hiss
Cease not, and change not, night nor day.
And moving at unheard commands,
The abysses and vast fires between,
Flit figures that with clanking hands
Obey a hideous routine;
They are not flesh, they are not bone,
They see not with the human eye,
And from their iron lips is blown
A dreadful and monotonous cry;
And whoso of our mortal race
Should find that city unaware,
Lean Death would smite him face to face,
And blanch him with its venomed air:

Or caught by the terrific spell,
Each thread of memory snapt and cut,
His soul would shrivel and its shell
Go rattling like an empty nut.

It was not always so, but once,
In days that no man thinks upon,
Fair voices echoed from its stones,
The light above it leaped and shone:
Once there were multitudes of men,
That built that city in their pride,
Until its might was made, and then
They withered age by age and died.
But now of that prodigious race,
Three only in an iron tower,
Set like carved idols face to face,
Remain the masters of its power;
And at the city gate a fourth,
Gigantic and with dreadful eyes,
Sits looking toward the lightless north.
Beyond the reach of memories;
Fast rooted to the lurid floor,
A bulk that never moves a jot,
In his pale body dwells no more,
Or mind or soul—an idiot!
But sometime in the end those three
Shall perish and their hands be still,
And with the master's touch shall flee
Their incommunicable skill.
A stillness absolute as death
Along the slacking wheels shall lie,
And, flagging at a single breath,
The fires that moulder out and die.
The roar shall vanish at its height,
And over that tremendous town
The silence of eternal night
Shall gather close and settle down.
All its grim grandeur, tower and hall,
Shall be abandoned utterly,
And into rust and dust shall fall
From century to century;
Nor ever living thing shall grow,
Nor trunk of tree, nor blade of grass;
No drop shall fall, no wind shall blow,

Nor sound of any foot shall pass:
Alone of its accursèd state,
One thing the hand of Time shall spare,
For the grim Idiot at the gate
Is deathless and eternal there.

THE CLEARER SELF

BEFORE me grew the human soul,
And after I am dead and gone,
Through grades of effort and control
The marvellous work shall still go on.

Each mortal in his little span
Hath only lived, if he have shown
What greatness there can be in man
Above the measured and the known;

How through the ancient layers of night,
In gradual victory secure,
Grows ever with increasing light
The Energy serene and pure:

The Soul that from a monstrous past,
From age to age, from hour to hour,
Feels upward to some height at last
Of unimagined grace and power.

Though yet the sacred fire be dull,
In folds of thwarting matter furled,
Ere death be nigh, while life is full,
O Master Spirit of the world,

Grant me to know, to seek, to find,
In some small measure though it be,
Emerging from the waste and blind,
The clearer self, the grander me!

PERSONALITY

O DIFFERING human heart,
Why is it that I tremble when thine eyes,
Thy human eyes and beautiful human speech,
Draw me, and stir within my soul
That subtle ineradicable longing
For tender comradeship?
It is because I cannot all at once,
Through the half-lights and phantom-haunted mists
That separate and enshroud us life from life,
Discern the nearness or the strangeness of thy paths,
Nor plumb thy depths.
I am like one that comes alone at night
To a strange stream, and by an unknown ford
Stands, and for a moment yearns and shrinks,
Being ignorant of the water, though so quiet it is,
So softly murmurous,
So silvered by the familiar moon.

VOICES OF EARTH

WE HAVE not heard the music of the spheres,
The song of star to star, but there are sounds
More deep than human joy and human tears,
That Nature uses in her common rounds;
The fall of streams, the cry of winds that strain
The oak, the roaring of the sea's surge, might
Of thunder breaking afar off, or rain
That falls by minutes in the summer night.
These are the voices of earth's secret soul,
Uttering the mystery from which she came.
To him who hears them grief beyond control,
Or joy inscrutable without a name,
Wakes in his heart thoughts bedded there, impearled,
Before the birth and making of the world.

TO THE PROPHETIC SOUL

WHAT are these bustlers at the gate
Of now or yesterday,
These playthings in the hand of Fate,
That pass, and point no way;

These clinging bubbles whose mock fires
For ever dance and gleam,
Vain foam that gathers and expires
Upon the world's dark stream;

These gropers betwixt right and wrong,
That seek an unknown goal,
Most ignorant when they seem most strong;
What are they, then, O Soul,

That thou shouldst covet overmuch
A tenderer range of heart,
And yet at every dreamed-of-touch
So tremulously start?

Thou with that hatred ever new
Of the world's base control,
That vision of the large and true,
That quickness of the soul;

Nay, for they are not of thy kind,
But in a rarer clay
God dowered thee with an alien mind,
Thou canst not be as they.

Be strong, therefore; resume thy load,
And forward stone by stone
Go singing, though the glorious road
Thou travellest alone.

THE AUTUMN WASTE

THERE is no break in all the wide grey sky,
Nor light on any field, and the wind grieves
And talks of death. Where cold grey waters lie
Round greyer stones, and the new-fallen leaves
Heap the chill hollows of the naked woods,
A lisping moan, an inarticulate cry,
Creeps far among the charnel solitudes,
Numbing the waste with mindless misery.
In these bare paths, these melancholy lands,
What dream, or flesh, could ever have been young?
What lovers have gone forth with linkèd hands?
What flowers could ever have bloomed, what birds have sung?
Life, hopes, and human things seem wrapped away,
With shrouds and spectres, in one long decay.

WINTER EVENING

TONIGHT the very horses springing by
Toss gold from whitened nostrils. In a dream
The streets that narrow to the westward gleam
Like rows of golden palaces; and high
From all the crowded chimneys tower and die
A thousand aureoles. Down in the west
The brimming plains beneath the sunset rest,
One burning sea of gold. Soon, soon shall fly
The glorious vision, and the hours shall feel
A mightier master; soon from height to height,
With silence and the sharp unpitying stars,
Stern creeping frosts, and winds that touch like steel,
Out of the depth beyond the eastern bars,
Glittering and still shall come the awful night.

LET US be much with Nature; not as they
That labour without seeing, that employ
Her unloved forces, blindly without joy;
Nor those whose hands and crude delights obey
The old brute passion to hunt down and slay;
But rather as children of one common birth,
Discerning in each natural fruit of earth
Kinship and bond with this diviner clay.
Let us be with her wholly at all hours,
With the fond lover's zest, who is content
If his ear hears, and if his eye but sees;
So shall we grow like her in mould and bent,
Our bodies stately as her blessèd trees,
Our thoughts as sweet and sumptuous as her flowers

SALVATION

NATURE hath fixed in each man's life for dower
One root-like gift, one primal energy,
Wherefrom the soul takes growth, as grows a tree,
With sap and fibre, branch and leaf and flower;
But if this seed in its creative hour
Be crushed and stifled, only then the shell
Lifts like a phantom falsely visible,
Wherein is neither growth, nor joy, nor power.
Find thou this germ, and find thou thus thyself,
This one clear meaning of the deathless I,
This bent, this work, this duty—for thereby
God numbers thee, and marks thee for His own:
Careless of hurt, or threat, or praise, or pelf,
Find it and follow it, this, and this alone!

TO A MILLIONAIRE

THE WORLD in gloom and splendour passes by,
And thou in the midst of it with brows that gleam,
A creature of that old distorted dream
That makes the sound of life an evil cry.
Good men perform just deeds, and brave men die,
And win not honour such as gold can give,
While the vain multitudes plod on, and live,
And serve the curse that pins them down: But I
Think only of the unnumbered broken hearts,
The hunger and the mortal strife for bread,
Old age and youth alike mistaught, misfed,
By want and rags and homelessness made vile,
The griefs and hates, and all the meaner parts
That balance thy one grim misgotten pile.

THE MODERN POLITICIAN

WHAT manner of soul is his to whom high truth
Is but the plaything of a feverish hour,
A dangling ladder to the ghost of power?
Gone are the grandeurs of the world's iron youth,
When kings were mighty, being made by swords.
Now comes the transit age, the age of brass,
When clowns into the vacant empires pass,
Blinding the multitude with specious words.
To them faith, kinship, truth and verity,
Man's sacred rights and very holiest thing,
Are but the counters at a desperate play,
Flippant and reckless what the end may be,
So that they glitter, each his little day,
The little mimic of a vanished king.

DEATH

I LIKE to stretch full-length upon my bed,
Sometimes, when I am weary body and mind,
And think that I shall some day lie thus, blind
And cold, and motionless, my last word said.
How grim it were, how piteous to be dead!
And yet how sweet, to hear no more, nor see,
Sleeping, past care, through all eternity,
With clay for pillow to the clay-cold head.
And I should seem so absent, so serene:
They who should see me in that hour would ask
What spirit, or what fire, could ever have been
Within that yellow and discoloured mask;
For there seems life in lead, or in a stone,
But in a soul's deserted dwelling none.

UPLIFTING

WE PASSED heart-weary from the troubled house,
Where much of care and much of strife had been,
A jar of tongues upon a petty scene;
And now as from a long and tortured drouse,
The dark returned us to our purer vows:
The open darkness, like a friendly palm,
And the great night was round us with her calm:
We felt the large free wind upon our brows,
And suddenly above us saw revealed
The holy round of heaven—all its rime
Of suns and planets and its nebulous rust—
Sable and glittering like a mythic shield,
Sown with the gold of giants and of time,
The worlds and all their systems but as dust.

3

THERE is a beauty at the goal of life,
A beauty growing since the world began,
Through every age and race, through lapse and strife
Till the great human soul complete her span.
Beneath the waves of storm that lash and burn,
The currents of blind passion that appal,
To listen and keep watch till we discern
The tide of sovereign truth that guides it all;
So to address our spirits to the height,
And so attune them to the valiant whole,
That the great light be clearer for our light,
And the great soul the stronger for our soul:
To have done this is to have lived, though fame
Remember us with no familiar name.

AT THE LONG SAULT: MAY, 1660 *

UNDER the day-long sun there is life and mirth
In the working earth,
And the wonderful moon shines bright
Through the soft spring night,
The innocent flowers in the limitless woods are springing
Far and away
With the sound and the perfume of May,
And ever up from the south the happy birds are winging,
The waters glitter and leap and play
While the grey hawk soars.
But far in an open glade of the forest set
Where the rapid plunges and roars,
Is a ruined fort with a name that men forget—
A shelterless pen
With its broken palisade,
Behind it, musket in hand,
Beyond message or aid
In this savage heart of the wild,
Mere youngsters, grown in a moment to men,
Grim and alert and arrayed,

The comrades of Daulac stand.
Ever before them, night and day,
The rush and skulk and cry
Of foes, not men but devils, panting for prey;
Behind them the sleepless dream
Of the little frail-walled town, far away by the plunging stream,
Of maiden and matron and child,
With ruin and murder impending, and none but they
To beat back the gathering horror
Deal death while they may,
And then die.

Day and night they have watched while the little plain
Grew dark with the rush of the foe, but their host
Broke ever and melted away, with no boast
But to number their slain;
And now as the days renew
Hunger and thirst and care
Were they never so stout, so true,
Press at their hearts; but none
Falters or shrinks or utters a coward word,
Though each setting sun
Brings from the pitiless wild new hands to the Iroquois horde,
And only to them despair.

Silent, white-faced, again and again
Charged and hemmed round by furious hands,
Each for a moment faces them all and stands
In his little desperate ring; like a tired bull moose
Whom scores of sleepless wolves, a ravening pack,
Have chased all night, all day
Through the snow-laden woods, like famine let loose;
And he turns at last in his track
Against a wall of rock and stands at bay;
Round him with terrible sinews and teeth of steel
They charge and recharge; but with many a furious plunge and
        wheel,
Hither and thither over the trampled snow,
He tosses them bleeding and torn;
Till, driven, and ever to and fro
Harried, wounded and weary grown,
His mighty strength gives way
And all together they fasten upon him and drag him down.

So Daulac turned him anew
With a ringing cry to his men
In the little raging forest glen,
And this terrible sword in the twilight whistled and slew.
And all his comrades stood
With their backs to the pales, and fought
Till their strength was done;
The thews that were only mortal flagged and broke
Each struck his last wild stroke,
And they fell one by one,
And the world that had seemed so good
Passed like a dream and was naught.

And then the great night came
With the triumph-songs of the foe and the flame
Of the camp-fires.
Out of the dark the soft wind woke,
The song of the rapid rose alway
And came to the spot where the comrades lay,
Beyond help or care,
With none but the red men round them
To gnash their teeth and stare.

All night by the foot of the mountain
The little town lieth at rest,
The sentries are peacefully pacing;
And neither from East nor from West

Is there rumour of death or of danger;
None dreameth tonight in his bed
That ruin was near and the heroes
That met it and stemmed it are dead.

But afar in the ring of the forest,
Where the air is so tender with May
And the waters are wild in the moonlight
They lie in their silence of clay.

The numberless stars out of heaven
Look down with a pitiful glance;
And the lilies asleep in the forest
Are closed like the lilies of France.

*Written in 1898

84

Duncan Campbell Scott

you had two girls—Baptiste—
One is Virginie—
Hold hard—Baptiste!
Listen to me.

The whole drive was jammed
In that bend at the Cedars,
The rapids were dammed
With the logs tight rammed
And crammed; you might know
The Devil had clinched them below.

We worked three days—not a budge,
"She's as tight as a wedge, on the ledge,"
Says our foreman;
"Mon Dieu! boys, look here,
We must get this thing clear."
He cursed at the men
And we went for it then;
With our cant-dogs arow,
We just gave he-yo-ho;
When she gave a big shove
From above.

The gang yelled and tore
For the shore,
The logs gave a grind
Like a wolf's jaws behind,
And as quick as a flash,
With a shove and a crash,
They were down in a mash,
But I and ten more,
All but Isaàc Dufour,
Were ashore.

He leaped on a log in the front of the rush,
And shot out from the bind
While the jam roared behind;
As he floated along
He balanced his pole
And tossed us a song.

But just as we cheered,
Up darted a log from the bottom,
Leaped thirty feet square and fair,
And came down on his own.

He went up like a block
With the shock,
And when he was there
In the air,
Kissed his hand
To the land;
When he dropped
My heart stopped,
For the first logs had caught him
And crushed him;
When he rose in his place
There was blood on his face.

There were some girls, Baptiste,
Picking berries on the hillside,
Where the river curls, Baptiste,
You know—on the still side
One was down by the water,
She saw Isaàc
Fall back.

She did not scream, Baptiste,
She launched her canoe;
It did seem, Baptiste,
That she wanted to die too,
For before you could think
The birch cracked like a shell
In that rush of hell,
And I saw them both sink—

Baptiste!—
He had two girls,
One is Virginie,
What God calls the other
Is not known to me.

OTTAWA

CITY about whose brow the north winds blow,
Girdled with woods and shod with river foam,
Called by a name as old as Troy or Rome,
Be great as they, but pure as thine own snow;
Rather flash up amid the auroral glow,
The Lamia city of the northern star,
Than be so hard with craft or wild with war,
Peopled with deeds remembered for their woe.

Thou art too bright for guile, too young for tears,
And thou wilt live to be too strong for Time;
For he may mock thee with his furrowed frowns,
But thou wilt grow in calm throughout the years,
Cinctured with peace and crowned with power sublime,
The maiden queen of all the towered towns.

THE ONONDAGA MADONNA

SHE STANDS full-throated and with careless pose,
This woman of a weird and waning race,
The tragic savage lurking in her face,
Where all her pagan passion burns and glows;
Her blood is mingled with her ancient foes,
And thrills with war and wildness in her veins;
Her rebel lips are dabbled with the stains
Of feuds and forays and her father's woes.

And closer in the shawl about her breast,
The latest promise of her nation's doom,
Paler than she her baby clings and lies,
The primal warrior gleaming from his eyes;
He sulks, and burdened with his infant gloom,
He draws his heavy brows and will not rest.

THE PIPER OF ARLL

THERE was in Arll a little cove
Where the salt wind came cool and free:
A foamy beach that one would love,
If he were longing for the sea.

A brook hung sparkling on the hill,
The hill swept far to ring the bay;
The bay was faithful, wild or still,
To the heart of the ocean far away.

There were three pines above the comb
That, when the sun flared and went down,
Grew like three warriors reaving home
The plunder of a burning town.

A piper lived within the grove,
Tending the pasture of his sheep;
His heart was swayed with faithful love,
From the springs of God's ocean clear and deep

And there a ship one evening stood,
Where ship had never stood before;
A pennon bickered red as blood,
An angel glimmered at the prore.

About the coming on of dew,
The sails burned rosy, and the spars
Were gold, and all the tackle grew
Alive with ruby-hearted stars.

The piper heard an outland tongue,
With music in the cadenced fall;
And when the fairy lights were hung,
The sailors gathered one and all,

And leaning on the gunwales dark,
Crusted with shells and dashed with foam,
With all the dreaming hills to hark,
They sang their longing songs of home.

When the sweet airs had fled away,
The piper, with a gentle breath,
Moulded a tranquil melody
Of lonely love and longed-for death.

When the fair sound began to lull,
From out the fireflies and the dew,
A silence held the shadowy hull,
Until the eerie tune was through.

Then from the dark and dreamy deck
An alien song began to thrill;
It mingled with the drumming beck,
And stirred the braird upon the hill.

Beneath the stars each sent to each
A message tender, till at last
The piper slept upon the beach,
The sailors slumbered round the mast.

Still as a dream till nearly dawn,
The ship was bosomed on the tide;
The streamlet, murmuring on and on,
Bore the sweet water to her side.

Then shaking out her lawny sails,
Forth on the misty sea she crept;
She left the dawning of the dales,
Yet in his cloak the piper slept.

And when he woke he saw the ship,
Limned black against the crimson sun;
Then from the disc he saw her slip,
A wraith of shadow—she was gone.

He threw his mantle on the beach,
He went apart like one distraught,
His lips were moved—his desperate speech
Stormed his inviolable thought.

He broke his human-throated reed,
And threw it in the idle rill;
But when his passion had its mead,
He found it in the eddy still.

He mended well the patient flue,
Again he tried its varied stops;
The closures answered right and true,
And starting out in piercing drops,

A melody began to drip
That mingled with a ghostly thrill
The vision-spirit of the ship,
The secret of his broken will.

Beneath the pines he piped and swayed,
Master of passion and of power;
He was his soul and what he played,
Immortal for a happy hour.

He, singing into nature's heart,
Guiding his will by the world's will,
With deep, unconscious, childlike art
Had sung his soul out and was still.

And then at evening came the bark
That stirred his dreaming heart's desire;
It burned slow lights along the dark
That died in glooms of crimson fire.

The sailors launched a sombre boat,
And bent with music at the oars;
The rhythm throbbing every throat,
And lapsing round the liquid shores,

Was that true tune the piper sent,
Unto the wave-worn mariners,
When with the beck and ripple blent
He heard that outland song of theirs.

Silent they rowed him, dip and drip,
The oars beat out an exequy,
They laid him down within the ship,
They loosed a rocket to the sky.

It broke in many a crimson sphere
That grew to gold and floated far,
And left the sudden shore-line clear,
With one slow-changing, drifting star

Then out they shook the magic sails,
That charmed the wind in other seas,
From where the west line pearls and pales,
They waited for a ruffling breeze.

But in the world there was no stir,
The cordage slacked with never a creak,
They heard the flame begin to purr
Within the lantern at the peak.

They could not cry, they could not move,
They felt the lure from the charmed sea;
They could not think of home or love
Or any pleasant land to be.

They felt the vessel dip and trim,
And settle down from list to list;
They saw the sea-plain heave and swim
As gently as a rising mist.

And down so slowly, down and down,
Rivet by rivet, plank by plank;
A little flood of ocean flown
Across the deck, she sank and sank.

From knee to breast the water wore,
It crept and crept; ere they were ware
Gone was the angel at the prore,
They felt the water float their hair.

They saw the salt plain spark and shine,
They threw their faces to the sky;
Beneath a deepening film of brine
They saw the star-flash blur and die.

She sank and sank by yard and mast,
Sank down the shimmering gradual dark;
A little drooping pennon last
Showed like the black fin of a shark.

And down she sank till, keeled in sand,
She rested safely balanced true,
With all her upward gazing band,
The piper and the dreaming crew.

And there, unmarked of any chart,
In unrecorded deeps they lie,
Empearled within the purple heart
Of the great sea for aye and aye.

Their eyes are ruby in the green
Long shaft of sun that spreads and rays,
And upward with a wizard sheen
A fan of sea-light leaps and plays.

Tendrils of or and azure creep,
And globes of amber light are rolled,
And in the gloaming of the deep
Their eyes are starry pits of gold.

And sometimes in the liquid night
The hull is changed, a solid gem,
That glows with a soft stony light,
The lost prince of a diadem.

And at the keel a vine is quick,
That spreads its bines and works and weaves
O'er all the timbers veining thick
A plenitude of silver leaves.

THE CUP

HERE is pleasure; drink it down.
Here is sorrow; drain it dry.
Tilt the goblet, don't ask why.
Here is madness; down it goes.
Here's a dagger and a kiss,
Don't ask what the reason is.
Drink your liquor, no one knows;
Drink it bravely like a lord,
Do not roll a coward eye,
Pain and pleasure is one sword
Hacking out your destiny;
Do not say, "It is not just."
That word won't apply to life;
You must drink because you must;

Tilt the goblet, cease the strife.
Here at last is something good,
Just to warm your flagging blood.
Don't take breath—
At the bottom of the cup
Here is death:
Drink it up.

THE SEA BY THE WOOD

I DWELL in the sea that is wild and deep,
But afar in a shadow still,
I can see the trees that gather and sleep
In the wood upon the hill.

The deeps are green as an emerald's face,
The caves are crystal calm,
But I wish the sea were a little trace
Of moisture in God's palm.

The waves are weary of hiding pearls,
Are aweary of smothering gold,
They would all be air that sweeps and swirls
In the branches manifold.

They are weary of laving the seaman's eyes
With their passion prayer unsaid,
They are weary of sobs and the sudden sighs
And movements of the dead.

All the sea is haunted with human lips
Ashen and sere and grey,
You can hear the sails of the sunken ships
Stir and shiver and sway,

In the weary solitude;
If mine were the will of God, the main
Should melt away in the rustling wood
Like a mist that follows the rain.

But I dwell in the sea that is wild and deep
And afar in the shadow still,
I can see the trees that gather and sleep
In the wood upon the hill.

THE WOOD BY THE SEA

I DWELL in the wood that is dark and kind
But afar off tolls the main,
Afar, far off I hear the wind,
And the roving of the rain.

The shade is dark as a palmer's hood,
The air with balm is bland:
But I wish the trees that breathe in the wood
Were ashes in God's hand.

The pines are weary of holding nests,
Are aweary of casting shade;
Wearily smoulder the resin crests
In the pungent gloom of the glade.

Weary are all the birds of sleep,
The nests are weary of wings,
The whole wood yearns to the swaying deep,
The mother of restful things.

The wood is very old and still,
So still when the dead cones fall,
Near in the vale or away on the hill,
You can hear them one and all,

And their falling wearies me;
If mine were the will of God—O, then
The wood should tramp to the sounding sea,
Like a marching army of men!

But I dwell in the wood that is dark and kind,
Afar off tolls the main;
Afar, far off I hear the wind
And the roving of the rain.

THEY dogged him all one afternoon,
Through the bright snow,
Two whitemen servants of greed;
He knew that they were there,
But he turned not his head;
He was an Indian trapper;
He planted his snow-shoes firmly,
He dragged the long toboggan
Without rest.

The three figures drifted
Like shadows in the mind of a seer;
The snow-shoes were whisperers
On the threshold of awe;
The toboggan made the sound of wings,
A wood-pigeon sloping to her nest.

The Indian's face was calm.
He strode with the sorrow of fore-knowledge,
But his eyes were jewels of content
Set in circles of peace.

They would have shot him;
But momently in the deep forest,
They saw something flit by his side:
Their hearts stopped with fear.
Then the moon rose.
They would have left him to the spirit,

But they saw the long toboggan
Rounded well with furs,
With many a silver fox-skin,
With the pelts of mink and of otter.
They were the servants of greed;
When the moon grew brighter
And the spruces were dark with sleep,
They shot him.
When he fell on a shield of moonlight
One of his arms clung to his burden;
The snow was not melted:
The spirit passed away.

Then the servants of greed
Tore off the cover to count their gains;
They shuddered away into the shadows,
Hearing each the loud heart of the other.
Silence was born.

There in the tender moonlight,
As sweet as they were in life,
Glimmered the ivory features,
Of the Indian's wife.

In the manner of Montagnais women
Her hair was rolled with braid;
Under her waxen fingers
A crucifix was laid.

He was drawing her down to the Mission,
To bury her there in spring,
When the bloodroot comes and the windflower
To silver everything.

But as a gift of plunder
Side by side were they laid,
The moon went on to her setting
And covered them with shade.

THE FORSAKEN

1

ONCE in the winter
Out on a lake
In the heart of the north-land,
Far from the Fort
And far from the hunters,
A Chippewa woman
With her sick baby,
Crouched in the last hours
Of a great storm.
Frozen and hungry,
She fished through the ice
With a line of the twisted
Bark of the cedar,

And a rabbit-bone hook
Polished and barbed;
Fished with the bare hook
All through the wild day,
Fished and caught nothing;
While the young chieftain
Tugged at her breasts,

Or slept in the lacings
Of the warm *tikanagan*.
All the lake-surface
Streamed with the hissing
Of millions of iceflakes
Hurled by the wind;
Behind her the round
Of a lonely island
Roared like a fire
With the voice of the storm
In the deeps of the cedars.
Valiant, unshaken,
She took of her own flesh,
Baited the fish-hook,
Drew in a grey-trout,
Drew in his fellows,
Heaped them beside her,
Dead in the snow.
Valiant, unshaken,
She faced the long distance,
Wolf-haunted and lonely,
Sure of her goal
And the life of her dear one:
Tramped for two days,
On the third in the morning,
Saw the strong bulk
Of the Fort by the river,
Saw the wood-smoke
Hang soft in the spruces,
Heard the keen yelp
Of the ravenous huskies
Fighting for whitefish:
Then she had rest.

Years and years after,
When she was old and withered,
When her son was an old man
And his children filled with vigour,
They came in their northern tour on the verge of winter,
To an island in a lonely lake.
There one night they camped, and on the morrow
Gathered their kettles and birch-bark
Their rabbit-skin robes and their mink-traps,
Launched their canoes and slunk away through the
    islands,
Left her alone forever,
Without a word of farewell,
Because she was old and useless,
Like a paddle broken and warped,
Or a pole that was splintered.
Then, without a sigh,
Valiant, unshaken,
She smoothed her dark locks under her kerchief,
Composed her shawl in state,
Then folded her hands ridged with sinews and corded
    with veins,
Folded them across her breasts spent with the nourishing
    of children,
Gazed at the sky past the tops of the cedars,
Saw two spangled nights arise out of the twilight,
Saw two days go by filled with the tranquil sunshine,
Saw, without pain, or dread, or even a moment of long-
    ing:
Then on the third great night there came thronging and
    thronging
Millions of snowflakes out of a windless cloud;
They covered her close with a beautiful crystal shroud,
Covered her deep and silent.
But in the frost of the dawn,
Up from the life below,
Rose a column of breath
Through a tiny cleft in the snow,
Fragile, delicately drawn,
Wavering with its own weakness,
In the wilderness a sign of the spirit,
Persisting still in the sight of the sun
Till day was done.

Then all light was gathered up by the hand of God and
    hid in His breast,
Then there was born a silence deeper than silence,
Then she had rest.

SPRING ON MATTAGAMI

FAR in the east the rain-clouds sweep and harry,
Down the long haggard hills, formless and low,
Far in the west the shell-tints meet and marry,
Piled grey and tender blue and roseate snow;
East—like a fiend, the bolt-breasted, streaming
Storm strikes the world with lightning and with hail;
West—like the thought of a seraph that is dreaming,
Venus leads the young moon down the vale.

Through the lake furrow between the gloom and bright'n-
    ing
Firm runs our long canoe with a whistling rush,
While Potàn the wise and the cunning Silver Lightning
Break with their slender blades the long clear hush;
Soon shall I pitch my tent amid the birches,
Wise Potàn shall gather boughs of balsam fir,
While for bark and dry wood Silver Lightning searches;
Soon the smoke shall hang and lapse in the moist air.

Soon shall I sleep—if I may not remember
One who lives far away where the storm-cloud went;
May it part and starshine burn in many a quiet ember,
Over her towered city crowned with large content;
Dear God, let me sleep, here where deep peace is,
Let me own a dreamless sleep once for all the years,
Let me know a quiet mind and what heart ease is,
Lost to light and life and hope, to longing and to tears.

Here in the solitude less her memory presses,
Yet I see her lingering where the birches shine,
All the dark cedars are sleep-laden like her tresses,
The gold-moted wood-pools pellucid as her eyen;
Memories and ghost-forms of the days departed

People all the forest lone in the dead of night;
While Potàn and Silver Lightning sleep, the happy-
    hearted,
Troop they from their fastnesses upon my sight.

Once when the tide came straining from the Lido,
In a sea of flame our gondola flickered like a sword,
Venice lay abroad builded like beauty's credo,
Smouldering like a gorget on the breast of the Lord:
Did she mourn for fame foredoomed or passion shattered
That with a sudden impulse she gathered at my side?
But when I spoke the ancient fates were flattered,
Chill there crept between us the imperceptible tide.

Once I well remember in her twilight garden,
She pulled a half-blown rose, I thought it meant for me,
But poising in the act, and with half a sigh for pardon,
She hid it in her bosom where none may dare to see:
Had she a subtle meaning?—would to God I knew it,
Where'er I am I always feel the rose leaves nestling there,
If I might know her mind and the thought which then
    flashed through it,
My soul might look to heaven not commissioned to
    despair.

Though she denied at parting the gift that I besought
    her,
Just a bit of ribbon or a strand of her hair;
Though she would not keep the token that I brought her.
Proud she stood and calm and marvellously fair;
Yet I saw her spirit—truth cannot dissemble—
Saw her pure as gold, staunch and keen and brave,
For she knows my worth and her heart was all atremble,
Lest her will should weaken and make her heart a slave.

If she could be here where all the world is eager
For dear love with the primal Eden sway,
Where the blood is fire and no pulse is thin or meagre,
All the heart of all the world beats one way!
There is the land of fraud and fame and fashion,
Joy is but a gaud and withers in an hour,
Here is the land of quintessential passion,
Where in a wild throb Spring wells up with power.

She would hear the partridge drumming in the distance,
Rolling out his mimic thunder in the sultry noons;
Hear beyond the silver reach in ringing wild persistence
Reel remote the ululating laughter of the loons;
See the shy moose fawn nestling by its mother,
In a cool marsh pool where the sedges meet;
Rest by a moss-mound where the twin-flowers smother
With a drowse of orient perfume drenched in light and
    heat:

She would see the dawn rise behind the smoky mountain,
In a jet of colour curving up to break,
While like spray from the iridescent fountain,
Opal fires weave over all the oval of the lake:
She would see like fireflies the stars alight and spangle
All the heaven meadows thick with growing dusk,
Feel the gipsy airs that gather up and tangle
The woodsy odours in a maze of myrrh and musk:

There in the forest all the birds are nesting,
Tells the hermit thrush the song he cannot tell,
While the white-throat sparrow never resting,
Even in the deepest night rings his crystal bell:
O, she would love me then with a wild elation,
Then she must love me and leave her lonely state,
Give me love yet keep her soul's imperial reservation,
Large as her deep nature and fathomless as fate:

Then, if she would lie beside me in the even,
On my deep couch heaped of balsam fir,
Fragrant with sleep as nothing under heaven,
Let the past and future mingle in one blur;
While all the stars were watchful and thereunder
Earth breathed not but took their silent light,
All life withdrew and wrapt in a wild wonder
Peace fell tranquil on the odorous night:

She would let me steal—not consenting or denying—
One strong arm beneath her dusky hair,
She would let me bare, not resisting or complying,
One sweet breast so sweet and firm and fair;
Then with the quick sob of passion's shy endeavour,
She would gather close and shudder and swoon away,
She would be mine for ever and for ever,
Mine for all time and beyond the judgement day.

Vain is the dream, and deep with all derision—
Fate is stern and hard—fair and false and vain—
But what would life be worth without the vision,
Dark with sordid passion, pale with wringing pain?
What I dream is mine, mine beyond all cavil,
Pure and fair and sweet, and mine for evermore,
And when I will my life I may unravel,
And find my passion dream deep at the red core.

Venus sinks first lost in ruby splendour,
Stars like wood-daffodils grow golden in the night,
Far, far above, in a space entranced and tender,
Floats the growing moon pale with virgin light.
Vaster than the world or life or death my trust is
Based in the unseen and towering far above;
Hold me, O Law, that deeper lies than Justice,
Guide me, O Light, that stronger burns than Love.

THE HALF-BREED GIRL

SHE is free of the trap and the paddle,
The portage and the trail,
But something behind her savage life
Shines like a fragile veil.

Her dreams are undiscovered,
Shadows trouble her breast,
When the time for resting cometh
Then least is she at rest.

Oft in the morns of winter,
When she visits the rabbit snares,
An appearance floats in the crystal air
Beyond the balsam firs.

Oft in the summer mornings,
When she strips the nets of fish,
The smell of the dripping net-twine
Gives to her heart a wish.

But she cannot learn the meaning
Of the shadows in her soul,
The lights that break and gather,
The clouds that part and roll,

The reek of rock-built cities,
Where her fathers dwelt of yore,
The gleam of loch and shealing,
The mist on the moor,

Frail traces of kindred kindness,
Of feud by hill and strand,
The heritage of an age-long life
In a legendary land.

She wakes in the stifling wigwam,
Where the air is heavy and wild,
She fears for something or nothing
With the heart of a frightened child.

She sees the stars turn slowly
Past the tangle of the poles,
Through the smoke of the dying embers,
Like the eyes of dead souls.

Her heart is shaken with longing
For the strange, still years,
For what she knows and knows not,
For the wells of ancient tears.

A voice calls from the rapids,
Deep, careless and free,
A voice that is larger than her life
Or than her death shall be.

She covers her face with her blanket,
Her fierce soul hates her breath,
As it cries with a sudden passion
For life or death.

NIGHT BURIAL IN THE FOREST

LAY him down where the fern is thick and fair.
Fain was he for life, here lies he low:
With the blood washed clean from his brow and his beautiful hair,
Lay him here in the dell where the orchids grow.

Let the birch-bark torches roar in the gloom,
And the trees crowd up in a quiet startled ring
So lone is the land that in this lonely room
Never before has breathed a human thing.

Cover him well in his canvas shroud, and the moss
Part and heap again on his quiet breast,
What recks he now of gain, or love, or loss
Who for love gained rest?

While she who caused it all hides her insolent eyes
Or braids her hair with the ribbons of lust and of lies,
And he who did the deed fares out like a hunted beast
To lurk where the musk-ox tramples the barren ground
Where the stroke of his coward heart is the only sound.

Haunting the tamarac shade,
Hear them up-thronging
Memories foredoomed
Of strife and of longing:
Haggard or bright
By the tamaracs and birches,

Where the red torch light
Trembles and searches,
The wilderness teems
With inscrutable eyes
Of ghosts that are dreams
Commingled with memories.

Leave him here in his secret ferny tomb,
Withdraw the little light from the ocean of gloom,
He who feared naught will fear aught never,
Left alone in the forest forever and ever.

Then, as we fare on our way to the shore
Sudden the torches cease to roar :
For cleaving the darkness remote and still
Comes a wind with a rushing, harp-like thrill,
The sound of wings hurled and furled and unfurled,
The wings of the Angel who gathers the souls from the
      wastes of the world.

BY A CHILD'S BED

SHE breathèd deep,
And stepped from out life's stream
Upon the shore of sleep;
And parted from the earthly noise,
Leaving her world of toys,
To dwell a little in a dell of dream.

Then brooding on the love I hold so free,
My fond possessions come to be
Clouded with grief;
These fairy kisses,
This archness innocent
Sting me with sorrow and disturbed content:
I think of what my portion might have been,
A dearth of blisses,
A famine of delights,
If I had never had what now I value most;
Till all I have seems something I have lost;
A desert underneath the garden shows,
And in a mound of cinders roots the rose.

Here then I linger by the little bed,
Till all my spirit's sphere,
Grows one half brightness and the other dead,
One half all joy, the other vague alarms;
And, holding each the other half in fee,
Floats like the growing moon
That bears implicity
Her lessening pearl of shadow
Clasped in the crescent silver of her arms.

THE HEIGHT OF LAND

Here is the height of land:
The watershed on either hand
Goes down to Hudson Bay
Or Lake Superior;
The stars are up, and far away
The wind sounds in the wood, wearier
Than the long Ojibwa cadence
In which Potàn the Wise
Declares the ills of life
And Chees-que-ne-ne makes a mournful sound
Of acquiescence. The fires burn low
With just sufficient glow
To light the flakes of ash that play
At being moths, and flutter away
To fall in the dark and die as ashes:
Here there is peace in the lofty air,
And Something comes by flashes
Deeper than peace;—
The spruces have retirèd a little space
And left a field of sky in violet shadow
With stars like marigolds in a water-meadow.

Now the Indian guides are dead asleep;
There is no sound unless the soul can hear
The gathering of the waters in their sources.
We have come up through the spreading lakes
From level to level,—
Pitching our tents sometimes over a revel
Of roses that nodded all night,
Dreaming within our dreams,
To wake at dawn and find that they were captured
With no dew on their leaves;
Sometimes mid sheaves
Of bracken and dwarf-cornel, and again
On a wide blueberry plain
Brushed with the shimmer of a bluebird's wing;
A rocky islet followed
With one lone poplar and a single nest
Of white-throat-sparrows that took no rest
But sang in dreams or woke to sing,—

To the last portage and the height of land—:
Upon one hand
The lonely north enlaced with lakes and streams,
And the enormous targe of Hudson Bay,
Glimmering all night
In the cold arctic light;
On the other hand
The crowded southern land
With all the welter of the lives of men.
But here is peace, and again
That Something comes by flashes
Deeper than peace—a spell
Golden and inappellable
That gives the inarticulate part
Of our strange being one moment of release
That seems more native than the touch of time.
And we must answer in chime;
Though yet no man may tell
The secret of that spell
Golden and inappellable.

Now are there sounds walking in the wood,
And all the spruces shiver and tremble,
And the stars move a little in their courses.
The ancient disturber of solitude
Breathes a pervasive sigh,
And the soul seems to hear
The gathering of the waters at their sources;
Then quiet ensues and pure starlight and dark;
The region-spirit murmurs in meditation,
The heart replies in exaltation
And echoes faintly like an inland shell
Ghost tremors of the spell;
Thought reawakens and is linked again
With all the welter of the lives of men.
Here on the uplands where the air is clear
We think of life as of a stormy scene—
Of tempest, of revolt and desperate shock;
And here, where we can think, on the bright uplands
Where the air is clear, we deeply brood on life
Until the tempest parts, and it appears
As simple as to the shepherd seems his flock:
A Something to be guided by ideals—
That in themselves are simple and serene—

Of noble deed to foster noble thought,
And noble thought to image noble deed,
Till deed and thought shall interpenetrate,
Making life lovelier, till we come to doubt
Whether the perfect beauty that escapes
Is beauty of deed or thought or some high thing
Mingled of both, a greater boon than either:
Thus we have seen in the retreating tempest
The victor-sunlight merge with the ruined rain,
And from the rain and sunlight spring the rainbow.

The ancient disturber of solitude
Stirs his ancestral potion in the gloom,
And the dark wood
Is stifled with the pungent fume
Of charred earth burnt to the bone
That takes the place of air.
Then sudden I remember when and where—
The last weird lakelet foul with weedy growths
And slimy viscid things the spirit loathes,
Skin of vile water over viler mud
Where the paddle stirred unutterable stenches,
And the canoes seemed heavy with fear,
Not to be urged toward the fatal shore
Where a bush fire, smouldering, with sudden roar
Leaped on a cedar and smothered it with light
And terror. It had left the portage-height
A tangle of slanted spruces burned to the roots,
Covered still with patches of bright fire
Smoking with incense of the fragrant resin
That even then began to thin and lessen
Into the gloom and glimmer of ruin.
'Tis overpast. How strange the stars have grown;
The presage of extinction glows on their crests
And they are beautied with impermanence;
They shall be after the race of men
And mourn for them who snared their fiery pinions,
Entangled in the meshes of bright words.

A lemming stirs the fern and in the mosses
Eft-minded things feel the air change, and dawn
Tolls out from the dark belfries of the spruces.
How often in the autumn of the world
Shall the crystal shrine of dawning be rebuilt

With deeper meaning! Shall the poet then,
Wrapped in his mantle on the height of land,
Brood on the welter of the lives of men
And dream of his ideal hope and promise
In the blush sunrise? Shall he base his flight
Upon a more compelling law than Love
As Life's atonement; shall the vision
Of noble deed and noble thought immingled
Seem as uncouth to him as the pictograph
Scratched on the cave side by the cave-dweller
To us of the Christ-time? Shall he stand
With deeper joy, with more complex emotion,
In closer commune with divinity,
With the deep fathomed, with the firmament charted,
With life as simple as a sheep-boy's song,
What lies beyond a romaunt that was read
Once on a morn of storm and laid aside
Memorious with strange immortal memories?
Or shall he see the sunrise as I see it
In shoals of misty fire the deluge-light
Dashes upon and whelms with purer radiance,
And feel the lulled earth, older in pulse and motion,
Turn the rich lands and the inundant oceans
To the flushed color, and hear as now I hear
The thrill of life beat up the planet's margin
And break in the clear susurrus of deep joy
That echoes and reëchoes in my being?
O Life is intuition the measure of knowledge
And do I stand with heart entranced and burning
At the zenith of our wisdom when I feel
The long light flow, the long wind pause, the deep
Influx of spirit, of which no man may tell
The Secret, golden and inappellable?

SENZA FINE

THAT is the rain
Sobbing, sobbing
Against the window pane.
And the wind comes robbing
The rain of its voice

And leaves me no choice,
In the dead room,
But to hear the noise
Of my heart throbbing, throbbing.

But before the storm
The evening was warm
I remember, and calm,
And by the mill dam
The martins were flashing,
If she had not said—!
But then say it she did—
I should be rid
Of the throbbing, throbbing,
At the heart of the shadow
That stands by the window
Sobbing, sobbing,
And breathes the dark
And sucks at the noise
Like a vampire—hark!
Robbing, robbing
The storm of its voice.

The miller's children at play,
I remember, called to each other,
And I tried to smother
The sound of her words,
But then—what she showed me!
'Tis between her vest,
The one I gave on her birthday,
Crimson, with silver pomegranates,
And her breast:

They will find it there,
But what can they say?
They cannot find
What it did to my mind,
Or what she said
When she threw back her head
And smiled,
So maddening, so wild.

To the left of the trail
Through the beaver meadow,
An arm of the swale
Is bordered with iris,
And the ferns grow rank,
But nothing is dank,
Crisp, pungent, dry:
The wind lingers by,
And stops.
There may have been a few drops.

Throbbing, throbbing,
And there is the rain
Robbing, robbing
The wind of its voice,
And it beats again
On the window pane,
Sobbing, sobbing.

LILACS AND HUMMING BIRDS

LACE-LIKE in the moonlight,
The white lilac tree was quiet,
A little form of dream delight
Within a dreaming scene,
Like a little bride of shadow
In a dim secluded eyot,
With perfume for an element
Around the white and green.

The secret of this dream delight,
The core of this bride-quiet,
Hid even from the moonlight
By the heart-leaved screen,
Was the dew encrusted jewel
Of a ruby-throat, and nigh it
A nest of sleeping humming-birds
Amid the white and green.

A VISION

THE tenebrous sky
Was founded on lightning,
And there came marching
To a funeral,
A multitude so millioned
That number was unthinkable;
There were massed together
Kings pierced with their sceptres,
Tyrants shod with the points of swords,
And priests each with a live coal
In the palm of his hand,
Learned men
With book-yokes on their necks,
Merchants with gold eyelids;
Each one tortured with his symbol,
And an innumerable host
Without sign or distinction;
Each bore a tuft of grass
In his fingers;
The grass was in seed,
And as they walked,
The seed fell where it listed.
There was no sound
As the host marched
To the funeral;
But what was buried
Was far in the Past,
And the host poured up
From the Future.

POWASSAN'S DRUM

Throb—throb—throb—throb—
Is this throbbing a sound
Or an ache in the air?
Pervasive as light,
Measured and inevitable,

It seems to float from no distance,
But to live in the listening world—
Throb—throb—throb—throb—throbbing
The sound of Powassan's Drum.

He crouches in his dwarf wigwam
Wizened with fasting,
Fierce with thirst,
Making great medicine
In memory of hated things dead
Or in menace of hated things to come,
And the universe listens
To the throb—throb—throb—throb—
Throbbing of Powassan's Drum.

The world seems lost and shallow,
Seems sunken and filled with water,
With shores lightly moving
Of marish grass and slender reeds.
Through it all goes
The throbbing of Powassan's Drum.

Has it gone on forever,
As the pulse of Being?
Will it last till the world's end
As the pulse of Being?
He crouches under the poles
Covered with strips of birch-bark
And branches of poplar and pine,
Piled for shade and dying
In dense perfume,
With closed eyelids
With eyes so fierce,
Burning under and through
The ancient worn eyelids,
He crouches and beats his drum.

The morning star formed
Like a pearl in the shell of darkness;
Light welled like water from the springs of morning;
The stars in the earth shadow
Caught like whitefish in a net;

The sun, the fisherman,
Pulling the net to the shore of night,
Flashing with the fins of the caught stars—
All to the throbbing of Powassan's Drum.

The live things in the world
Hear it and are silent.
They hide silent and charmed
As if guarding a secret;
Charmed and silent hiding a rich secret,
Throbbing all to the
Throb—throb—throbbing of Powassan's Drum.

Stealthy as death the water
Wanders in the long grass,
And spangs of sunlight
Slide on the slender reeds
Like beads of bright oil.
The sky is a bubble blown so tense
The blue has gone grey
Stretched to the throb—throb—throb—throb—
Throbbing of Powassan's Drum.

Is it a memory of hated things dead
That he beats—famished—
Or a menace of hated things to come
That he beats—parched with anger
And famished with hatred—?

The sun waited all day.
There was no answer.
He hauled his net
And the glint of the star-fins
Flashed in the water of twilight;
There was no answer.
But in the northeast
A storm cloud reaches like a hand
Out of the half darkness.
The spectral fingers of cloud
Grope in the heavens,
And at moments, sharp as pain,
A bracelet of bright fire
Plays on the wrist of the cloud.
Thunder from the hollow of the hand
Comes almost soundless, like an air pressure,

And the cloud rears up
To the throbbing of Powassan's Drum.
An infusion of bitter darkness
Stains the sweet water of twilight.

Then from the reeds stealing,
A shadow noiseless,
A canoe moves noiseless as sleep,
Noiseless as the trance of deep sleep
And an Indian still as a statue,
Moulded out of deep sleep,
Headless, still as a headless statue,
Moulded out of deep sleep,
Sits modelled in full power,
Haughty in manful power,
Headless and impotent in power.
The canoe stealthy as death
Drifts to the throbbing of Powassan's Drum.
The Indian fixed like bronze
Trails his severed head
Through the dead water
Holding it by the hair,
By the plaits of hair,
Wound with sweet grass and tags of silver.
The face looks through the water
Up to its throne on the shoulders of power,
Unquenched eyes burning in the water,
Piercing beyond the shoulders of power
Up to the fingers of the storm cloud.
Is this the meaning of the magic—
The translation into sight
Of the viewless hate?
Is this what the world waited for
As it listened to the throb—throb—throb—throb—
Throbbing of Powassan's Drum?

The sun could not answer.
The tense sky burst and went dark
And could not answer.
But the storm answers.
The murdered shadow sinks in the water.
Uprises the storm
And crushes the dark world;
At the core of the rushing fury

Bursting hail, tangled lightning
Wind in a wild vortex
Lives the triumphant throb—throb—throb—throb—
Throbbing of Powassan's Drum.

AT GULL LAKE: AUGUST, 1810

GULL LAKE set in the rolling prairie—
Still there are reeds on the shore,
As of old the poplars shimmer
As summer passes;
Winter freezes the shallow lake to the core;
Storm passes,
Heat parches the sedges and grasses,
Night comes with moon-glimmer,
Dawn with the morning-star;
All proceeds in the flow of Time
As a hundred years ago.

Then two camps were pitched on the shore,
The clustered teepees
Of Tabashaw Chief of the Saulteaux;
And on a knoll tufted with poplars
Two grey tents of a trader—
Nairne of the Orkneys.
Before his tents under the shade of the poplars
Sat Keejigo, third of the wives
Of Tabashaw Chief of the Saulteaux;
Clad in the skins of antelopes
Broidered with porcupine quills
Coloured with vivid dyes,
Vermilion here and there
In the roots of her hair,
A half-moon of powder-blue
On her brow, her cheeks
Scored with light ochre streaks.
Keejigo daughter of Launay
The Normandy hunter
And Oshawan of the Saulteaux,
Troubled by fugitive visions
In the smoke of the camp-fires,

In the close dark of the teepee,
Flutterings of colour
Along the flow of the prairies,
Spangles of flower tints
Caught in the wonder of dawn,
Dreams of sounds unheard—
The echoes of echo,
Star she was named for
Keejigo, star of the morning,
Voices of storm—
Wind-rush and lightning—
The beauty of terror;
The twilight moon
Coloured like a prairie lily,
The round moon of pure snow,
The beauty of peace;
Premonitions of love and of beauty
Vague as shadows cast by a shadow.
Now she had found her hero,
And offered her body and spirit
With abject unreasoning passion,
As Earth abandons herself
To the sun and the thrust of the lightning.
Quiet were all the leaves of the poplars,
Breathless the air under their shadow,
As Keejigo spoke of these things to her heart
In the beautiful speech of the Saulteaux.

> The flower lives on the prairie,
> The wind in the sky,
> I am here my beloved;
> The wind and the flower.
>
> The crane hides in the sand-hills,
> Where does the wolverine hide?
> I am here my beloved,
> Heart's-blood on the feathers
> The foot caught in the trap.
>
> Take the flower in your hand,
> The wind in your nostrils;
> I am here my beloved;
> Release the captive,
> Heal the wound under the feathers.

A storm-cloud was marching
Vast on the prairie,
Scored with livid ropes of hail,
Quick with nervous vines of lightning—
Twice had Nairne turned her away
Afraid of the venom of Tabashaw,
Twice had the Chief fired at his tents
And now when two bullets
Whistled above the encampment
He yelled "Drive this bitch to her master."

Keejigo went down a path by the lake;
Thick at the tangled edges,
The reeds and the sedges
Were grey as ashes
Against the death-black water;
The lightning scored with double flashes
The dark lake-mirror and loud
Came the instant thunder.
Her lips still moved to the words of her music,
"Release the captive,
Heal the wound under the feathers."

At the top of the bank
The old wives caught her and cast her down
Where Tabashaw crouched by his camp-fire.
He snatched a live brand from the embers,
Seared her cheeks,
Blinded her eyes,
Destroyed her beauty with fire,
Screaming, "Take that face to your lover."
Keejigo held her face to the fury
And made no sound.
The old wives dragged her away
And threw her over the bank
Like a dead dog.

Then burst the storm—
The Indians' screams and the howls of the dogs
Lost in the crash of hail
That smashed the sedges and reeds,
Stripped the poplars of leaves,
Tore and blazed onwards,
Wasting itself with riot and tumult—
Supreme in the beauty of terror.

The setting sun struck the retreating cloud
With a rainbow, not an arc but a column
Built with the glory of seven metals;
Beyond in the purple deeps of the vortex
Fell the quivering vines of the lightning.
The wind withdrew the veil from the shrine of the moon,
She rose changing her dusky shade for the glow
Of the prairie lily, till free of all blemish of colour
She came to her zenith without a cloud or a star,
A lovely perfection, snow-pure in the heaven of midnight.
After the beauty of terror the beauty of peace.

But Keejigo came no more to the camps of her people;
Only the midnight moon knew where she felt her way,
Only the leaves of autumn, the snows of winter
Knew where she lay.

AT DELOS

AN IRIS-FLOWER with topaz leaves,
With a dark heart of deeper gold,
Died over Delos when light failed
And the night grew cold.

No wave fell mourning in the sea
Where age on age beauty had died;
For that frail colour withering away
No sea-bird cried.

There is no grieving in the world
As beauty fades throughout the years:
The pilgrim with the weary heart
Brings to the grave his tears.

1. Charles G. D. Roberts, 1860–1943.

Cappon, James, *Charles G. D. Roberts* (Toronto, 1925).

Roberts, Lloyd, *The Book of Roberts* (Toronto, 1923).

Pomeroy, E. M., *Sir Charles G. D. Roberts: A Biography* (Toronto, 1943).

Pacey, Desmond, "Sir Charles G. D. Roberts," *Ten Canadian Poets* (Toronto, 1958).

2. Bliss Carman, 1861–1929.

Cappon, James, *Bliss Carman and the Literary Currents and Influences of his Time* (Toronto, 1930).

MacKay, L. A., "Bliss Carman," *Canadian Forum* 13 : 182–3 (February 1933).

Ross, Malcolm, "Carman by the Sea," *Dalhousie Review* 27 : 294–298.

Shepard, Odell, *Bliss Carman* (Toronto, 1923).

Pacey, Desmond, "Bliss Carman," *Ten Canadian Poets* (Toronto, 1958).

3. Archibald Lampman, 1861–1899.

Brown, E. K., "Archibald Lampman," *On Canadian Poetry* (Toronto, 1944).

Collin, W. C., "Natural Landscape," *White Savannahs* (Toronto, 1936).

Gustafson, Ralph, "Among the Millet," *Northern Review* 1 : 26–34 (February–March 1947).

Beattie, Munro, "Archibald Lampman," *Our Living Tradition* (Toronto, 1957).

Pacey, Desmond, "Archibald Lampman," *Ten Canadian Poets* (Toronto, 1958).

4. Duncan Campbell Scott, 1862–1947.

Brown, E. K., "Duncan Campbell Scott," *On Canadian Poetry* (Toronto, 1944).

Smith, A. J. M., "The Poetry of Duncan Campbell Scott," *Dalhousie Review* 28 : 12–21 (April 1948).

Pacey, Desmond, "Duncan Campbell Scott," *Ten Canadian Poets* (Toronto, 1958).

INDEX OF TITLES

ARCHIBALD LAMPMAN

ARCHIBALD LAMPMAN

DUNCAN CAMPBELL SCOTT

THE POETS

SIR CHARLES G. D. ROBERTS was born in 1860 in New Brunswick and graduated from the University of New Brunswick in 1879. For ten years he taught at King's College, N.S., and in 1895 began his travels as a writer and an editor. He returned to Canada in 1925 and died here in 1943. He was a Fellow of the Royal Society of Canada and a Member of the Royal Society of Literature and the American Academy of Arts and Letters. In 1926 he was awarded the first Lorne Pierce Medal, and in 1935 had a knighthood conferred upon him.

BLISS CARMAN was born in Fredericton in 1861 and received his education at the universities of New Brunswick, Edinburgh, and Harvard. During his youth he engaged in teaching, law, and surveying, but the greater part of his life was devoted to editing, writing, and the pursuit of a philosophy based on a love of nature. He was made a corresponding member of the Royal Society of Canada, and received the Lorne Pierce Medal. After his death in 1929 he was posthumously awarded the medal of the Poetry Society of Canada.

ARCHIBALD LAMPMAN was born in Morpeth, Ontario in 1861. He graduated from Trinity College, University of Toronto in 1882. After a brief spell of teaching in 1883 he became clerk in the Post Office Department where he remained until his untimely death in 1899. During the remainder of his brief life he published many of his poems and two of his books, *Among the Millet* and *Lyrics of Earth*. *Alcyone* and *At the Long Sault* were published posthumously. In 1895 he was made Fellow of the Royal Society of Canada.

DUNCAN CAMPBELL SCOTT was born in 1862 in Ottawa. He was educated there and in Stanstead, and in 1879 entered the Department of Indian Affairs where, as an administrator, he acquired his wide knowledge and understanding of the Indians, and it was during this time also that he was drawn by Lampman into the writing of poetry. In 1890 he became a Fellow of the Royal Society of Canada of which he was president in 1921–22. He died in 1947, having written nine volumes of poetry and several prose works.